# $elling
## TO YOUR
# Grandmother

## IMAGINE IF YOU TREATED
## *EVERY CUSTOMER*
## LIKE YOU WOULD TREAT
## YOUR OWN GRANDMOTHER

## CHRIS COLTRAN

*DR DAVE CARPENTER*
*CHRIS COLTRAN*

### TRIBAL
**P R E S S**
San Antonio, Texas

*This publication is designed to give an accurate portrayal of the subject matter
covered. It is sold with the understanding that the publisher and author are not
engaged in rendering legal, accounting, or other professional service. If legal advice
or expert assistance is required, the services of a competent professional person
should be sought.*

**Published by
Tribal Press 2004
San Antonio, Texas**

ISBN: 09760156-0-9

**Printed in the United States of America**

*01*

**Library of Congress Cataloging-in-Publication Data**

Coltran, Chris.
Selling to Your Grandmother: Imagine treating every customer like you would treat
your own Grandmother / by Chris Coltran
p.    cm.
Includes index.
ISBN 09760156-0-9
1. Selling   2. Customer Service   3. Customer Loyalty
I. Coltran, Chris. II. Title.

Cover Concept & Design by John Guzman.
Interior Illustrations by Joel Barbee.

*To my sons, Dawson and Jacob,*
*who keep me young at heart and full of energy,*
*and to the only person who completes me,*
*my wife, Anna.*

# Contents:

# THE ESSENTIALS

# SELLING TO YOUR GRANDMOTHER

*Inspired by true stories and actual events.*

*All names have been changed for the privacy of the individuals depicted herein.*

## Preface to Selling to Your Grandmother

Selling your Grandmother can be done a number of ways, including a yard sale, a public auction, or with your computer on eBay. Of course, I am kidding. Either way, selling your Grandmother is illegal, and downright ridiculous. If you thought this was a way to get rid of your beloved Grandmother, you are wrong. Put this book back on the shelf, it is not for you. This is a book about sales. No matter what your profession, you are in sales. Whether you sell yourself to your employer, or sell goods or services to a consumer, you are a salesperson.

The original idea of *Selling to Your Grandmother* first came about while on a sales call. John, a customer and friend, asked the question, *"What would happen if a salesperson treated every customer as if he or she were their Grandmother?"* It seemed like such a simple concept at the time. Imagine how much differently you might treat a consumer if he or she were actually your Grandmother. If your Grandmother were shopping in your store, you would not even question whether she would buy from you or from someone else. It was just a matter of finding out what she was looking for, showing her all of her options, and writing up the sale. The more we talked about it, the more fun the topic became.

I began demonstrating what I was calling the *Grandmother Philosophy on Sales* in some of my sales presentations, and it did not take long until I had compiled quite a list of examples where this concept made sense. At the time, the *Grandmother Philosophy* was just a different approach to selling, not a book. However, after seeing firsthand how salespeople reacted to these simple questions, I realized I had a tool that was giving salespeople a new perspective on how to approach a sale. After some encouragement from colleagues, I decided to turn the

*Grandmother Philosophy* into a book. Because of the enjoyment I experienced while sharing this concept, it seemed this was the next logical step. Two years later, *Selling to Your Grandmother*, the book, was complete.

I have been in sales, both wholesale and retail, for the last 13 years. I would even venture to say that I have been in sales my whole life. At age fourteen, I put together a bicycle freestyle trick team. Five guys, including myself, would do tricks on our bikes choreographed to music at shopping malls, fairs, and other events. I was not much of a rider, so I declared myself the manager and announcer for the team. The following summer while on vacation, I went to Seattle to spend a few weeks with my Uncle Dave and Aunt Heidi. As my Uncle Dave recalls, it was that summer that I made my first official sales presentation. I had discovered that a major helmet and sunglass manufacturer had their corporate offices in Bellevue, Washington, just a few miles away from their home.

One afternoon, I had my Aunt drive me to the building where the office was located. I was just a kid, so I couldn't drive myself. Without an appointment, I walked in to meet with the national sales manager of the company. What were take action immediately to correct a problem to keep your customer happy. I would place a wager on the fact that some of the most successful salespeople have waited tables before graduating into sales. If you are someone who has never worked in the restaurant business, don't worry. A restaurant is just one place to find a good salesperson. Good salespeople come from all walks of life. After working in the food industry for six years, I traded in my apron and order pad for a commission sales job.

As a sales rep for a manufacturer, I am able to listen to and learn from hundreds of retail salespeople every day. These are the people working day in and day out, down in the trenches with the retail public. Whether I am doing a sales presentation or listening to a salesperson, I am always learning. I have found that a sale can actually be compared to a jigsaw puzzle. You can have all the pieces, but until they are assembled, you do not have a complete picture. However, once all the pieces have been put in place, the puzzle is complete. My point here is simple. To be successful in sales, you need to have all the pieces of the puzzle and know how they fit together.

For a long time, I felt that someone had to be born with the *"sales"* ability. You either have it, or you don't. I no longer, however, subscribe to this philosophy. I believe that anyone who has the desire and ambition to be in sales can achieve success. Although it may appear some salespeople have the golden touch, it is only the difference between having all the pieces to the puzzle and knowing how they fit together. If you have ever struggled, this book can help put those struggles behind you. If you are new to the sales profession, *Selling to Your Grandmother* will give you a head start on a successful selling career.

I believe everyone has been in sales their whole life. Think about it. You were in sales from the time you took your first breath. As soon as you were born, you cried your first cry, and your mother fed you. When you needed a new diaper, you sold your mother by fussing, and she changed it. When you wanted her to pick you up, all you had to do was make some noise, and up you went. By the time you were three years old, you were one of the best salespeople around. How about when you convinced your parents that you would do all of your chores around the house if they bought you a new bike? Or when you wanted to take the car out on your first date?

A receptionist at a dentist office is also a salesperson. If they are rude to the dentist's patients, those patients might lose their patience and find a new dentist. If a front desk clerk at a hotel is not friendly with hotel guests, the guests might decide to stay somewhere else on their next trip. A lawyer has to sell their client by convincing them they can win their case, and then they have to sell the jury. A doctor has to sell his or her patients on entrusting that he or she can diagnose their illness and make them well. A teacher has to sell their students on believing what they are teaching is important. An advertiser has to sell a consumer into thinking they need to purchase their product in their advertisement or commercial. A politician has to sell his or her constituents on entrusting them with their vote. A childcare provider has to sell parents on his or her ability to take good care of their children. A plastic surgeon has to sell his or her patients on their ability to fix their problem or to make them look better. An actor has to sell the audience on whether his or her performance is believable. A job applicant has to sell him or herself in an interview to get hired for a job. If you have a job, you are in sales.

Everyone is in sales. How about when you convinced your girlfriend that if she married you, she would never have to get a job? You probably convinced her you would buy her a big house, take her on exotic vacations every year, and live happily ever after. If you are married, you are in sales. If you have children, you are in sales. A person does not actually have to sell you something you can hold in your hands to be called a salesperson. I think you get the point. Whether you knew it or not, everyone has been in sales their whole life.

Maybe you are someone who is reading this book to help you decide whether or not you want to be a salesperson? We have already established that no matter what your profession, you are already in sales. The question is do you want to get paid like you are in sales? A commission sales job beats any hourly or salary position hands down. A salary position is a security blanket for a lot of people because they like knowing what their paycheck will be every two weeks. Sure, it is nice to know what you are going to get paid, but month after month, and year after year, the same paycheck doesn't usually motivate people to work very hard. It is easy to plan the family budget, but when the budget expands, the paycheck lags behind. When you work on commission, you are not limited by the number of hours in a week or your hourly wage. In sales there are no restrictions on how much money you can make, and the sky is the limit. Your commission amount may vary from month to month, but the more you sell, the more you will get paid. If you are ambitious, and not afraid of a challenge, you should not be afraid to work on commission.

Below are some of the questions I have been asking salespeople ever since I first started using the concept of *Selling to Your Grandmother*:

*If your Grandmother walked into your store, how would you greet her?*

*If your Grandmother walked into your store wearing torn up clothes and looking frazzled, would you prejudge her?*

*If your Grandmother walked into your store, would you try to up sell her?*

*Would you sell your Grandmother a product that you were not proud of or one that you would not buy for yourself?*

*How would you go the extra mile for your Grandmother?*

*If you were selling to your Grandmother, how would you close the sale?*

*Would you show your Grandmother all of your products even if you could not afford to buy them for yourself?*

*Would you keep it simple if your Grandmother walked into your store?*

*If your Grandmother walked into your store, would you have a good attitude?*

*If your Grandmother walked into your store, would you tell her the truth?*

*If your Grandmother walked into your store, how would you read her body language?*

*If your Grandmother walked into your store with a problem, how would you fix it?*

*If your Grandmother walked into your store, would she buy from you?*

*If your Grandmother made a purchase from you, would she be pleased enough to give you a referral?*

Each of these questions will be addressed in the following chapters. By answering them, my hope is to give you a new and simple way to approach a sale. *Selling to Your Grandmother* will offer something for everyone, both young and old. If you are a veteran salesperson, this will be a new twist. If you are just starting out, this will be one of many ways to help you succeed. *Selling to Your Grandmother* has some of my own personal experiences and many actual stories from salespeople I have worked with over the years. Remember, no two sales situations are ever the same. In fact, no two consumers are ever the same. What works with one consumer will not always work with another. My goal is for you to take these experiences and apply them to your selling. If you do, I believe you will become more successful and prosperous in your selling career.

Lastly, I wanted to say thank you to everyone who helped make this book possible. Without all the stories and experiences to draw from, it would have been impossible to write. Joel Barbee, who did the illustrations, was fantastic to work with. His talent is endless, and I cannot say enough about his contribution. The first day I started writing, I imagined having illustrations throughout the book, and they turned out exactly the way I had hoped. With *Selling to Your Grandmother* now complete, I could not imagine reading it without them. A special thank you to my wonderful wife, who had to listen to me bounce this idea around for years before finally deciding to write this book. Thank you for never letting me lose my focus.

Part I.

The
Sale

## The Introduction

You have probably heard the phrase, *"You only get one chance to make a good first impression."* It's true. Just like on a first date when you wanted him or her to think you were their perfect match. My first *real* date with my wife was to a nice romantic dinner. At the end of the evening, I thanked her for a wonderful time, and gave her a goodnight kiss on the back of her hand. It was one of those moments in time that I will never forget. Now that we have been married for five years, I asked her what might have happened had I tried to give her a real kiss on our first night out. She would be the first to tell you, if I had tried to kiss her on the lips, we would have never gone out again, and I would have been history. Wow! Talk about only one chance to make a good first impression.

When a potential customer walks into your store, what are you going to do? Consumers get so turned off when they walk into a store and a salesperson from across the room just looks up and does nothing. They might acknowledge their presence by nodding or smiling and then they let the customer roam around the store while they finish up what they were doing. Is what they are doing more important than a new customer? More important than what they might buy? Who knows? When I walk into a store and a salesperson ignores me or just looks up and smiles, he or she will not get the chance to find out. I will not make a purchase and give a commission to a salesperson that is below average. Don't forget that a consumer decides whether a salesperson gets a commission or not. How is this so, you ask? If a consumer does not like the salesperson they are dealing with, they have the choice to walk out of their store and buy from someone else. When a waitperson gives bad service, do you give them a tip? Not a very good one. Remember that your customer is the king of the sale. Treat them like royalty.

When a consumer walks in your door, get up and greet them. Walk up and say hello. Welcome them to your store and introduce yourself. Always put your hand out to a new client and give them a firm handshake. Repeat their name and say, *"Mike Jones, it's nice to meet you."* Repeating their name will help you in two ways. First, it will help you to remember it. Second, the most pleasant sound a person ever hears is his or her own name. If you do these two things, your customer will know you are listening and they will like what they are hearing. Whatever you do, **don't be average**. Try to have a few opening questions that require a real answer. One of my personal favorites is, *"What kind of project are you working on today?"* This is just one of many opening questions you can use with a new customer. If you have some favorites that work for you, keep using them. If not, try this one, or come up with some of your own that will work for the product you are selling.

Using the name of your customer is a good way to make your sale more personal, but be careful not to overuse it. Nothing is more annoying than a sales person who uses his or her clients name in every other sentence. Once or twice is plenty, especially after just meeting them. Overusing their name can make you look like you are trying too hard. A salesperson trying too hard to make a connection with their customer might appear pushy and fake, and most consumers tend to shy away from these kinds of people. Chances are, the more relaxed you are during the sale, the more business you are going to write up.

When I first started in sales, I needed help in breaking the ice. One method that worked well for me was to *FORM* my customers. **People would much rather talk about themselves** than talk about you, so don't be like one of those people who cannot wait for a chance to interrupt someone to talk about him or herself. I have seen how a person can turn someone off by always talking about their own life and never listening to someone else's. If you are one of these people, you will struggle to become a great salesperson. Don't do it. You might be surprised to find out how interesting other peoples lives are if you would only listen. Various network-marketing organizations teach their independent business owners to *FORM* their prospects. So if you have trouble talking with and getting to know your clients, try to *FORM* them. *FORM* is an acronym that stands for: *Family, Occupation, Recreation,* and *Message*. After you use it a few times, you really don't even have to think about it. The *FORM* method will start to happen naturally every time you meet new people.

*Family* is where someone is from, where they live now, where they went to school, whether they are single or married, and if they have children. Instead of using the same questions so many other salespeople ask to break the ice, I use these. I try to have a real conversation. I never ask questions that will have a *"Yes"* or *"No"* answer, and I try to make sure they require some thought. If I can have a conversation with them, there is a good chance I will find something in common to talk about. Ask about what their *Occupation* is. Not only will this give you an idea of what income level they are at, you might also find out you have something in common with one another. *Recreation* is an easy subject to bring up. Most people love to talk about what they do for fun, so ask them. This will give your customers even more time to talk about themselves. By using the *FORM* method, you have learned where your customer is from, what they do for a living, and what they do for entertainment. You are now ready to talk about the *Message*, which is the sale.

Other methods can also be used to start a conversation if you choose not to *FORM* your customers. You can start by taking notice of the clothes they are wearing. It might be a baseball hat, a t-shirt, or a company jacket with a business logo on it. Try to observe anything you can about your customer to see what you might have in common with one another. If you know someone who works where they work, mention it. It is a great icebreaker to talk about something you have in common with your customer. Try to make a personal connection as quickly as possible with a new client. The quicker you do, the better your chances will be for you to sell them something.

Chad has been in sales for 23 years, and he loves college football. In fact, I can't recall a conversation with him that we did not end up talking about the subject. I have watched him talk about football with many of his clients, as well. I don't think it is something he even thinks about, it just happens. If someone walks into his store with a college or university football hat or jacket on, it is an easy conversation for him to start, and it works quite well for him. Think about your interests and what you enjoy. Some of them could probably be used as conversation topics to help you make a connection with a potential client.

Todd, who sells sporting goods, also uses this technique to his advantage. He lives in an area where deer and elk hunting is very popular. He actually loves the sport and enjoys talking about it with his clients. It is a topic that he is very familiar with and knows a lot about, so it works great for him. I have seen him use this technique more times than I could count. Once he has made a connection with his client, he moves right into the selling process. The main reason this works for him is because he honestly loves to hunt. The topic of hunting, however, would not work if he did not know anything about the subject and only used it to start a conversation. Make sure when using this technique, you talk about a subject you are familiar with or have an interest in. Whatever you do, don't make up a story.

Another way to start a conversation might be to look at the vehicle your customer drove up in. They might be driving a pickup just like yours, so you can ask how they like their Chevy. Yes, it is small talk, but it works. It will make you and your client feel more comfortable with each other if you can find something you have in common. This, of course, only works if you can see the parking lot or the front of the store when they drive up. When using this technique, a fatal mistake is when a salesperson makes up a story. If a customer drives up with a pair of skis on the top of their car, a salesperson could start up a conversation about skiing. If you are going to use this technique, I recommend you make sure it is a real interest. Do not tell a customer you like to ski if you don't even like being in the snow. If your new client finds out you made up a story when you first met, they might also think you are making up a story about your product and trying to snow them. This will likely damage your credibility enough that your client will not trust you enough to do business with you now or in the future.

Although these techniques work most of the time, even the best salespeople will occasionally have a consumer who says, *"We're just looking."* This is one of the most dreaded phrases for a new salesperson to ever hear. Don't let yourself get hung up on it; because it is very unlikely your customer is only looking. The chances they are *"just looking"* or *"window shopping"* is slim, so whatever you do; do not believe them. Sure, it is possible someone is looking at the new cars on a car lot, or the new televisions in an electronics store, but it is highly unlikely they are *"just looking"* with no intention to buy. A consumer will usually say this as a defense mechanism, because they are either uncomfortable with you or the product they are looking at. As a salesperson, when someone says this to me, I always come back with the same response. I immediately reply, *"Great. You came to the right place. We get lots of people just looking in our store."* After pointing out the various departments, I tell them to take their time, and if they have any questions, to just ask. Here is an example of how one salesperson handled a customer who said she was *"just looking."*

Angela had just bought a new car and wanted her stereo to sound really good when she cruised down the road with her friends. She walked into a local stereo shop she had heard about from a friend. Within seconds of walking in the door, Dan walked up and asked what he could do for her.

Angela was definitely out of her comfort zone, so she said she was *"just looking."* He immediately welcomed her to his store and without even knowing what she was in the market for; he proceeded to show her all the different products they sell. He asked her to make herself at home and he would be back to check on her in a few minutes.

Dan walked back to his desk, and left Angela to start *"looking"* on her own. Since she was looking for car stercos, she headed in that direction. She started looking at all the different brands, models, and prices. Dan kept a close eye on her, but kept his distance until she looked toward him like she had a question and needed some assistance. This was his opening and he took it. He found out her car was a Honda Civic and he assured her that his store had installed numerous stereo systems into them. He proceeded to explain all the features and benefits of the different brands and models of car stereos. After finding out what she expected from a new stereo, and what she wanted to spend, they were able to select a model that met her expectations and her budget.

Angela had been to almost every stereo shop in town, and Dan was different than all the other salespeople she had encountered. Unlike the other salespeople, he allowed her time to get acclimated to his store before trying to sell her anything. When she told the other salespeople in the other stores she was *"just looking,"* most of them said something like, *"Great. Let me know if you need anything?"* They would then leave her alone to roam the store, until she eventually worked her way back toward the front door and walked out without making a purchase.

Dan did not make this common mistake. He knows that a person does not typically walk into a store only to look. They usually have a very good reason for braving the traffic, parking their car, and walking into his store. He took the necessary time to allow Angela to get comfortable in her new environment. After she was comfortable, he began to show her all of her options. Car stereos can be very confusing to someone who has never bought one before, and when a consumer is uncomfortable with their level of knowledge or experience with a product, they are usually apprehensive. They also may not trust the salesperson quite yet, and may not be ready to spend their money either. Dan was able to take his customer from *"just looking"* into selling her a new stereo system and having it installed into her car.

Every person who has ever worked in sales will tell you how important it is to be able to read body language. Without saying a word, people are talking with their bodies loud and clear. A salesperson needs to constantly be observing what their client's body language is saying to them. It could be how a consumer is standing or the expression on their face. In fact, one of the best indicators of how your customer perceives you is to look into their eyes. Some people are so good at talking with their eyes; they could probably stroll through life without ever speaking a word. Because every part of your customer's body is talking, you need to pay attention to it and figure out what it is telling you.

Sometimes people do not always get along with certain people, and it is okay. **It would be nice to get along with everyone you meet, but it is just not possible.** At some point, you may encounter a consumer who might not like you because of the way you look. Maybe you resemble someone they dislike or you remind them of someone who cut them off in traffic? Whatever the reason, it just is not possible to get along with everyone. A consumer who is *"just looking"* might be one of those people. If you have given them time to acclimate to your store, and they still will not give you the time of day, don't fret. Read their body language. What is it saying? Go with your gut and do not be afraid to trust your instincts. If it looks like they don't like you or are uncomfortable with you, you are probably right. In this situation, your customer is certainly going to walk out without buying from you or your store.

IT WOULD BE NICE TO GET ALONG WITH EVERYONE, BUT IT IS JUST NOT POSSIBLE.

Whatever you do, don't let your store lose the sale. Make sure if you are not going to get the sale, someone from your store does. Grab another salesperson and introduce them to your customer. Walk away and leave the other salesperson to see if they can break the ice and get past whatever your barrier was with them. Do not feel bad if they make the sale and the commission, because each sale your store gets is one less sale for the store down the street. It does not matter whether you or a fellow salesperson closes a sale, as long as they are buying from your store. Don't be selfish. The same salesperson you gave a customer to will eventually repay you by passing you one of their customers when they are unable to make a connection. What comes around usually goes around.

While on a sales call, I watched a salesperson make an excellent first impression with some new clients. Jeff, who has worked in sales for the last 15 years, worked with a brand new customer who had just walked into his store looking for new floor coverings for their entire home. Minutes before, Jeff and I were just discussing how far behind he was with his paperwork. He could have kept to it when Dan and Vicki walked in, but he didn't. He stood up and greeted his new potential clients within seconds of them walking in the door. He introduced himself and asked about their project they were working on. After a few more probing questions, he started the selling process. He was visibly excited and genuinely interested in his new clients project. Jeff could have easily kept to his paperwork and not even bothered getting up from his desk. After all, there were two other salespeople in the store that could have helped them.

He spent almost two hours with them helping make their selections, and by not allowing his paperwork to hold him down; he picked up a new client. Jeff was a veteran salesperson who knew the importance of making a good first impression and not letting anything keep him from new customers. Once Dan and Vicki's house was completed, the sale totaled just over $12,000. You will only get one chance to work with a new client and to make a good first impression. Do not blow the opportunity by worrying about things that can be done anytime. A salesperson cannot pick and choose when a new customer walks into their store. You can only work with a new customer when you have one, so stand up and work with a customer every time one walks in the door.  Remember, if you don't work with them, someone else will.

**If your Grandmother walked into your store, how would you greet her?**  You should never let anything come between you and your customer, especially if that customer is your Grandmother.  Don't even for a minute let her walk around your store before greeting her.  Get up out of your desk and say hello the moment she walks in the door.  If you hesitate, another salesperson might beat you to her.  Would you allow another salesperson to sell to your Grandmother?  The best time to work with a new customer is when they are in your store; your paperwork and phone calls can wait.  Normally you might *FORM* your customer to break the ice, and get them to talk about him or herself.  Pay attention to their attire, or what they drove up in, to help guide you with your questions.  If you sense some uneasiness with your customer, let them get acclimated to your store before going any further.  Do not forget how to handle someone who is *"just looking."*  You might first catch up on recent family events, and then find out what your Granny is looking for.  If you imagine your next customer is your Grandmother, you will see how much easier it will be to make a good first impression and connection with them.

# Prejudging

Imagine a consumer who walks into your store wearing jeans and a t-shirt. If you don't help them because you are too busy with better looking prospects, watch out. We have all been taught not to be prejudice against people who are different than ourselves. If you judge a potential client based on their appearance, you are guilty. **If you prejudge, you are going to fail.** If you don't believe me, try it and see for yourself that prejudging is like committing sales suicide. This reminds me of a time when I bought a new car.

I was driving by a car dealership, when I saw a white sports car that had grabbed my attention. I had broken my leg a few weeks before, and was currently on crutches. I was wearing shorts, a sweatshirt, a baseball hat, and probably looked like I was seventeen years old. After checking out the car for some time, I actually had to hobble into the dealership to ask someone for help. If this were to happen again, I would definitely leave and take my business elsewhere. Four salespeople were on the floor, and I was the only customer on the lot. It was a cold and rainy November day, and they obviously did not want to leave their cozy desks and their hot coffee for a kid looking at a car he could not afford. Or so they thought? I should have left, but I really wanted to take it for a test drive. Finally a young, rookie salesperson asked if he could help me. I heard the veteran salespeople grumble, thinking he was wasting his time. After all, this kid could not afford a sports car. I assume they had made a judgment based on my appearance. I sure proved them wrong.

Three veteran salespeople passed on my appearance as well as a commission. I wanted to laugh at them for how stupid they were for judging a customer based on their appearance. Instead, I waived at them as they watched a kid who could not afford a new car drive one off the lot.

I have never forgotten this experience of being prejudged by a salesperson. If you remember in the movie classic, *Pretty Woman*, Julia Roberts was treated poorly when she first tried to go shopping in Beverly Hills. She was dressed like a streetwalker and looked as though she could not afford those ritzy stores, so the salesladies refused to help her. With some help from Richard Gere, and his credit cards, she was able to find a store that would help her. The salespeople all worked on commission and knew he had a lot of money to spend. Wasn't it great when Julia Roberts returned to the stores that had prejudged her the day before to show them all the bags of her expensive purchases?

By prejudging her, those salesladies made a big mistake and missed out on a lot of commissions. If a salesperson prejudges a customer, I refer to it as the *Pretty Woman Syndrome.* With the level of professionalism increasing in the sales industry, a sales person who prejudges is going to fail. Do not hinder your sales by thinking someone either has or does not have money based on their appearance. This is the best way to lose a ton of business, so don't fall into this trap. People do not wear a sign around their neck that says they are wealthy. In fact, people with money tend to look the same as people without money. Sure, there are always exceptions, but I have met many wealthy people who look like an average Joe walking down the street.

So how do you know what to look for?  The vehicle they are driving?  The jewelry they are wearing?  The way they talk?  The clothes they are wearing?  Wait a minute! Did you not hear me?  I said never prejudge.  Period.  I don't know how to spell it out any more clearly.  Ask a successful veteran salesperson who has been selling for many years how he or she prejudges a consumer.  The answer is always the same, *"they don't."*

The easiest way to see how people prejudge is to simply go out to dinner.  I have proven this theory by accident many times.  Pick a restaurant, and it does not have to be expensive.  The first time you dine, make sure you are wearing a business suit or a nice shirt and slacks.  Order dinner like you normally would, and I am sure the service is going to be excellent.  Your waitperson will probably make sure your water glass is never empty and that your meal is prepared just the way you ordered it.  You will basically get the service you have come to expect from a full service restaurant.  Now, the next day, around the same time, go back wearing a baseball hat and jeans.  I can almost guarantee your service will not be nearly as good as it was the day before. Remember a waitperson is also a salesperson. They will probably prejudge you based on your appearance and give their best service to the tables they think will leave them the best tips.

One night after a long day of sales calls, I checked into a hotel and changed into some comfortable clothes. I headed to dinner wearing jeans and a t-shirt. I felt the service was adequate, and my waitress received an average tip for average service. I realized how I had been prejudged based on my appearance when I went back the following evening to again have dinner. This time I didn't change out of my business suit after working all day. I actually had the same waitress and she did not even recognize me from the night before. The service was so much better; I thought I was dining in a different restaurant. If you have experienced this for yourself, you know what I mean. If not, try it. The experience will give you even more reason not to prejudge your own customers.

A friend of mine who sold cars once told me a story about the first Lexus he ever sold. A woman drove onto his lot in an old pickup with a rack in the back and paint all over the sides. She had paint on her overalls, in her hair, on her face, and even in her eyelashes. This was the first real sales job of Jim's life and he had only been working the floor for one month. When no other salespeople stepped up to help her, he walked outside to introduce himself. After 45 minutes, he walked inside and wrote up the sale of a brand new Lexus. Imagine the faces on the other salespeople when they realized what had just taken place. Jim said it was priceless. The woman had a girlfriend who had bought the same make of car and she had wanted one too. Not only did she buy the car on the spot, she paid with a check.

I asked Jim what made him get up and talk to her in the first place. He said because he was the new guy on the sales floor, the veterans all looked at him like you better go and talk to her because we aren't going to. He recalled how he had thought to himself on his way outside that he had a better chance selling something while talking to a potential customer than he did standing inside, talking to his fellow salespeople. He learned a very valuable lesson that day. Regardless of the situation, never make a prejudgment based on the appearance of a customer. Today, he no longer sells cars, but now lives in Seattle selling real estate.

I understand it is human nature to judge someone based on his or her appearance. We all know the first thing we see in a person is what they look like, but rarely admit it. We notice their clothes, their hair, the way they talk, as well as many other characteristics. There are so many different looking people in this world that it is difficult to judge someone based on their appearance alone. You cannot even assume that just because a person looks like a different nationality, does not mean they are not just as much of an American as you are. They may have actually been born in the same hospital as you were, and speak better English than yourself. I know it is difficult to see someone in ripped jeans and a t-shirt and think that he or she is wealthy, but you never know. When people are working, they wear their work clothes. When people are not working, they usually want to relax and dress casual.

Carl works in a bank as a financial advisor. He deals with clients of all sizes and with various backgrounds, ranging from a few thousand to multi-million dollar accounts. He told me of an experience he had with a new client who walked in off the street without a referral. Mrs. Berger asked if Carl could help her roll an old 401k into a traditional IRA. This was something he had done early in his career when he was trying to build up his portfolio, and the day she walked into his office, he was swamped with work.

Once he realized what she wanted to do and saw the dollar amount on her 401k was only seven thousand dollars, he didn't even want to waste his time. A fitting example for this book, it just so happened that Mrs. Berger was old enough to be Carl's Grandmother. He was actually ready to give her a name and number of someone else who would be able to help her. Although he should have helped her regardless of the dollar amount, he knew the paperwork alone was not even worth the commission on the transfer.

He recalled the main reason he decided to help her was because she reminded him of his own Grandmother. He asked himself, *"What kind of Grandson would send his own Grandma down the street to his competition?"* An hour later, Mrs. Berger walked out of the bank. With her transfer complete, Carl didn't give her another thought.

Four months had passed when Mrs. Berger walked back into Carl's office, once again with another investment she needed help with. He immediately started regretting even helping her in the first place. Now he would be forced to help her again and waste more of his time. He, of course, was pleasant with her and asked what she needed today. She pulled out her paperwork and showed him that she had over a half-million dollars in assets she wanted him to reinvest for her. Carl was almost speechless. When Mrs. Berger had first walked into his office, she looked like your average Grandmother you would see walking down the street. He later came to find out that she was a multi-millionaire. Who would have thought? A simple mistake four months ago had almost cost him $500,000 in his portfolio. Carl said this was the last time he has ever prejudged a potential client.

*If your Grandmother walked into your store wearing torn up clothes and looking frazzled, would you prejudge her?* No matter what your Grandmother looks like when she walks into your store, you are still going to treat her like you would treat your own Granny. It doesn't matter whether she looks like she worked all day in her garden, or if she is wearing her best church dress. Even if she drove up in a beat up vehicle, you would still give her the respect she deserves. Just because her hair might look purple, doesn't mean her wallet isn't green. She is there to spend some money no matter what she looks like, and you have no way of knowing how much money she has in her purse, or how much she is willing to spend. Anytime you catch yourself prejudging a consumer, just remember the *Pretty Woman Syndrome*. Successful salespeople do not prejudge their customers. Now think about all the possible situations you can encounter on the sales floor. Now imagine that all those customers' are your Grandmother. How are you going to treat the next consumer who walks into your store? Just like your Grandmother, of course.

## Up Selling

Up Selling is a concept that most people, both consumers and salespeople, do not fully understand. Think back to the last time you were shopping for something that required dealing with a commission salesperson. It could have been for a pair of shoes, a television, a new appliance, new furniture, or even a new vehicle. Chances are the salesperson tried to up sell you to a better product. To a consumer, up selling is something a salesperson does to get them to spend more money. To a salesperson, up selling increases their commission. To the storeowner, up selling raises the average selling price and helps increase the bottom line. With that being said, these are not the most important reasons for up selling a consumer. Up selling actually benefits everyone involved in the sale. In this chapter, we will discuss why up selling is so important and why a salesperson should always attempt to up sell every consumer to better products and services.

People tend to do business with people they know, and **anyone you come in contact with, even in leisure, is a potential customer.** Years ago when I was a bachelor, I decided it was time to buy a new sofa, so I jumped in the car and headed to the only furniture store where I personally knew a salesperson.

A few years earlier, I had sold Dale some building materials when he was remodeling his house. At the time, he appeared honest and I enjoyed working with him. When it came to buying a sofa, he was the only person who came to mind. There is a good point here about always being nice to people.  Here was a guy that I had come in contact with a few years before, and he was the only person I thought of when I needed to buy a new piece of furniture.  I walked into Dale's store to find him standing behind the sales counter.  I told him I was in the market for a new sofa.  At this point in my life, I really didn't know much about furniture.  This was not a problem because I expected to be educated by Dale on what to look for.  In fact, most consumers expect a salesperson to educate them on the products they are looking to purchase.

I walked around the store looking at his huge selection and sat on a few models to see how they felt.  Finally, a green, tan, and burgundy plaid sectional had caught my eye. I liked the recliners on each end that would be great for relaxing in front of the television.  Once he saw I was interested in it, he did not bother to show me anything else. He wrote up the sale and my purchase was complete.  He closed an easy sale and he was probably quite proud of himself.  If only he had tried to *sell* me a sofa instead of letting me *buy* one.  A good salesperson knows the difference.  Dale made the common mistake of a salesperson letting a customer *buy* something.  Yes, I said mistake.  If you are thinking a salesperson's job is to sell stuff, you are right.  The mistake was that he did not try to *sell* me anything.  He didn't show me any of my options, and he did not try to up sell me into anything else in the store.  He simply let me *buy* the first thing I showed any interest in.

After my new sofa was delivered to my house, I realized it looked a lot better on the showroom floor than it did in my living room.  Sure it was nicer than what I had replaced, but it was not the nicest sofa I could have purchased.  Over the next few years, the fabric began to show wear and the cushions started to break down.  The arms were not real sturdy and if you sat on them just right you might actually damage them.  When I was shopping for a new sofa, I was not shopping for the best price.  Dale did not show me the differences in quality of constructions, and he didn't try to up sell me into a better product.  He took the easy road by selling me the first sofa I showed any interest in.  He did not *sell* me a sofa; he simply let me *buy* one.  Maybe it was the jeans and t-shirt I was wearing?  Had he prejudged me?  He did not know how much money I made.  He sure didn't know what I was willing to spend on a new sofa.  Maybe he should have spent a little more time in the introductory phase?  If he would have found out what I did for a living, he may have realized he could have tried to sell me a more expensive item.  He let me *buy* the first thing my eyes were attracted to.  He blew it, and here's why.

Years later, my wife and I were shopping for new furniture for the addition we had added on to our home. The last time I had bought furniture was the sectional I had purchased from Dale. Surprise! Dale wasn't even a consideration. He did, in fact, come to mind, but only as a reminder to not shop at his store. No referral business for him.

Referrals will be discussed in more detail in chapter 14. Anyway, we needed a sofa, loveseat, and end tables, so we went to a store that had a reputation of selling nice furniture. I also heard they were expensive. Good. At least I knew we would not get another sofa like the one I had bought from Dale. I told my wife that she could have whatever she wanted and asked that she leave the negotiating up to me. Michelle greeted us and seemed very interested in our needs. She actually had a lot of veteran salesperson qualities. She first spent time in the introduction phase trying to gather some personal information about us. By asking the right questions, she was able to find out that my wife was a stay at home mom and that I was in sales. With these two facts alone, she was probably able to determine an approximate income bracket. Once she had some information to go on, she started to walk us through the entire store. She started at the leather sofas, showing us the most expensive to the least expensive. After the sofas, we looked at loveseats, again starting with the best ones first, then to the coffee and end tables.

Michelle had shown us all of our options from the most expensive to the sale items. She had asked about our project and appeared genuinely interested. She asked my wife questions about the colors she liked and what kind of theme she was looking for. Our first impressions were good, and she definitely did not prejudge us. In fact, she showed us furniture that was well out of our budget. She started high, and came down. We also felt she gave us enough technical information on the furniture we were looking at to make an educated decision, so we made our purchase. The new furniture was delivered to our home and we have been pleased with it ever since.

A year later, my wife and I were shopping for a new bed and mattress, so we went back to see Michelle. We loved what we had bought from her a year earlier, so we headed straight to her store. She was again a professional and started off by first showing us the top of the line mattresses. We looked at the middle range and Michelle insisted that we lay on the more expensive beds. This time we settled on a top of the line, king size, pillow-top mattress. A few months later, we headed back to the same store to look at beds for our two year old son. To our surprise, Michelle was no longer working at our favorite furniture store. Guess what? We still bought a bed at the same store, even though Michelle no longer worked there. We just had to find a new salesperson we were comfortable doing business with, and we made our purchase.

It is a fact that people do not work for the same company for 40 years and retire anymore. According to the U.S. Bureau of Labor Statistics, the average American has more than 9.6 jobs in their lifetime, and 52% of people starting a new job last less than one year. Even more alarming, 85% of employees last less than five years at a job before moving on to another company. This is why it is extremely important for an owner or store manager to make sure their salespeople are always trying to up sell to better products. Why? Because up selling will keep your customers coming back, year after year. Even if you have different people on your sales staff, your past customers will undoubtedly shop your store first. If you let your salespeople sell lower end, cheap products, you usually will not have to worry about past customers giving you any repeat business. Chances are if a consumer buys a low quality product, they will be unhappy with their purchase and will decide to shop elsewhere in the future. This is why up selling will keep repeat business walking through your door, long after a salesperson may have moved on to another line of work. A customer will be a customer for life if they are satisfied with their purchase, and up selling your customers to better products will help insure their satisfaction.

When Dale had sold me a sofa, he blew it. Yes, he did get my business, but only once. How much furniture can a person buy in their lifetime? He did not try to up sell me into a higher quality sofa when I could have probably purchased almost anything on the sales floor. Dale lost and so did his store. When I was in the market to buy more furniture, I did not even consider buying from him again. I also never considered the store he worked at. Both the store and salesperson lost. I went to a store that had a reputation of quality products and quality salespeople. To this day, each time we need to purchase a new piece of furniture, we keep going back to our favorite store. If a salesperson is always selling cheap products, his or her customers are more likely to be dissatisfied with their purchase. If they are dissatisfied with their purchase, consumers will usually hold it against the salesperson and the store, and choose not to shop there in the future.

The price a consumer pays for something always seems to be an important factor during a sale. However, consumers never seem to remember when they get a deal on something, or when they buy the sale item. A year or two after a purchase, most consumers usually even forget what they paid. They do, however, remember how it performs and how long it lasts. If they are unhappy with the performance of a product, they will likely not buy from the same salesperson ever again. They will also likely shop at a different store altogether. I cannot state it any more eloquently than a sign hanging behind a sales counter that read, *"The bitterness of poor quality lingers long after the sweetness of a low price."* A store is hurt by a salesperson not up selling because a consumer will hold the store responsible for selling them a cheap product. Even though the store had lots of quality products, the salesperson took the easy road, and never tried to *sell* them. So always remember that **a good salesperson will always *sell* something instead of letting a consumer *buy* something.**

Up selling is a good thing, as long as you do it for the right reasons. It needs to be in the best interest of your customer, and nothing to do with your commission check. You want your clients to buy the best product they can afford, and it is your job to make sure they know what they are purchasing. If your client cannot afford something, or it simply is not in their budget, they will tell you. A good salesperson will always try and up sell their customers to make sure they will be satisfied with their purchase.

Sure, it is one thing when a consumer does not want to purchase a higher quality product. It is their choice. If they have been shown all the products available and they choose a lower end model, at least they know what they are buying.

In my case, where I bought the first sofa I looked at, Dale did not try to up sell me into something better. I was unhappy with my purchase and held the store and salesperson accountable. A sales person who sells like this is unlikely to be successful in a long-term sales career. They are only looking at their commission check for this month and not worried about five or ten years down the road. They should be looking at the big picture and thinking long-term. When a salesperson sells a better product and their customer is satisfied, they are more likely to purchase again from the same salesperson. If it so happens that a salesperson has quit working at a store when a returning customer walks in, that consumer is still more likely to do business with the same store. They will just have to find a new salesperson they are comfortable doing business with.

Occasionally, a consumer will know exactly what they want to buy when they walk into your store. It is your job to make sure your customer is given every option before making their purchase, and to make sure they buy a product that is going to perform to their expectations. If they tell you they already know what they want to buy, be careful. If you have two different brands of a product that are of equal quality and equal price, is it worth trying to convince your customer to buy one brand over the other? Unless you think they are making a mistake by purchasing a particular brand, **don't try and reinvent the wheel**. If they prefer one brand over the other because a friend has the same, or they researched it on the Internet, why try and change their mind? If you try to hard to convince them to buy your personal favorite, you just might push them out of your store without selling them anything.

Brad has been selling jewelry for the last three years and it did not take him long to figure out how important it was to up sell his customers. Unlike a house, a vehicle, or food, jewelry is not a necessity. It is something that a person can live without. Easy for me to say, I'm a guy. I do not know too many women who would say they could live without it.  Most of the time, jewelry is purchased for a Wedding, Birthday, Anniversary, Christmas, or another special occasion.  Because there are over 360 other days left in the year, a jewelry salesperson needs to take advantage of up selling all of their customers.  Let's face it; jewelry can be complicated and confusing.  Most consumers do not know about gem quality, size of the stone, or the type of gold.  However, the one thing consumers do know about jewelry is, the more they spend, the nicer it tends to look.

Brad has found that most consumers who are buying jewelry are usually buying it because of the way it makes them feel when they are wearing it.  Most men would rather have their wife wearing a two-carat diamond ring than a one-carat, and Brad makes sure when a customer is trying on wedding rings; they try on most of them.  If they start out looking at $2000 rings, he keeps showing them more expensive ones.  Each time they are getting higher in quality and more beautiful than the one before.  Because most consumers buy jewelry on emotion, it is usually quite easy to up sell them into the better, more expensive items.  Once a ring is on their finger, it is hard for them to go back to one that does not look as nice or is smaller.  As long as he continues to up sell, Brad will always have satisfied customers who will give him repeat business for many years to come.

**If your Grandmother walked into your store, would you try to up sell her?** Your customer is expecting you to be an expert on the products you are selling, and so is your Grandmother. A salesperson needs to be able to give enough information to a consumer for them to be able to make an educated buying decision. If Granny wants to buy the first thing that catches her eye, it doesn't necessarily make it the right product for her. You owe it to your customer to show them the features and benefits of all the products you are selling. Some products are better than others, and it is up to you to make sure they are educated on the differences. Don't forget that the salesperson, the consumer, and the storeowner all benefit from up selling. If you up sell your customers to better products, you will be more likely to do business with them again in the future, and have a customer for life. Satisfied customers equal more referrals. More referrals equal more sales, and more sales equal higher commissions. So the next time you are up selling a customer, treat him or her like you would treat your own Grandmother and try to sell them the best product you can.

## Owning Your Product

At this point, you have been through the introductions with your new client. You have made a good first impression and have been anything but average. You have also discovered some things you have in common with one another. You *FORM'ed* them and found out that you maybe went to the same high school, or have children around the same age. You may have both worked in the same line of work, or have a friend in common. You may have also found out that you both enjoy hiking, fishing, or some other type of recreational activity. You have found out these things by using the *FORM* method or by just being observant and asking the right questions. Either way, you have made great strides with your new client, and you have separated yourself from your competition. Chances are very good that your client has not encountered another sales person who has been able to make a connection as quickly or smoothly as you have. You have also avoided prejudging your customer in any way. As far as you are concerned, your client can afford anything you have for sale. You are going to give them every possible option for their purchase by up selling them into better products.

You are now actually through the toughest part of the sale, and now comes the fun part. All successful salespeople take a genuine interest in their client's project, and you need to do the same. Your main goal is no longer to find things in common with one another, because you have already accomplished that. You have achieved a level of trust with your client, and it is safe to move to the next step. The sale now focuses on your client's project.

Shane works for a very large homebuilder in Atlanta and is responsible for meeting with new clients who are planning to build a new home. His company does not get involved in average houses, with his average price starting around one million dollars. It goes without saying that his clients all have a lot of money, and they are definitely in a position to choose whether Shane's company builds their home or one of his competitors. Although he does not personally build the homes, he is responsible for showing his clients exactly what his company can build for them. First, he sits down with his clients and collects ideas on what they want in their new home. They decide on the style of home, the design of the building, the windows, doors, woodwork, cabinetry, lighting, and everything else down to the smallest details. They go through numerous catalogs and idea books to help paint a mental picture of the home they are designing. Shane has a passion for what he does, and his clients can see his genuine love for homebuilding. After meeting with a client, he meets with architects and designers to put together a set of plans. Drawings of the home are presented to the buyer; changes are made and sent back to the drawing board. This process can sometimes take months, while numerous drawings and plans are drawn and re-drawn, until the buyer approves a final house plan.

During this process, Shane has to stay excited. Even if he is on the fourth drawing and six months have passed since the initial visit, he must remain excited about the project. If it appears to his client that he has lost interest, he runs the risk of losing them to one of his competitors. You can imagine that people with enough money to build a second or third home can be a little difficult to deal with at times. Even though he sometimes feels like pulling his hair out, he always keeps a mental picture of success in his head. His vision of success helps keep him from worrying about all the steps it takes to achieve it. Success is when Shane and his client are able to walk through a home that they created on paper and his company has built to perfection.

If you are selling houses for a living, you need to have a genuine interest for real estate. If you sell cooking utensils, you should enjoy spending time in the kitchen. The most successful salespeople have a personal interest in what they sell, and believe it or not, your clients can actually tell whether you enjoy the business you are in. Maybe you work at a Harley-Davidson motorcycle shop. If you do, I hope you own a Harley. If you don't, you should. How can you sell Harley's if you are pushing a moped down the sidewalk? You need to be able to convey the feeling of owning a Harley and what it feels like cruising down the highway to your customers. If you believe in the products you sell, you should own them. If you do own them, your customers will know that you are genuinely interested in your products, as well as their sale.

By owning the product or service you are trying to sell, you will have a much easier time convincing your customer that they should own it too. If you would not buy a product you are selling, you need to evaluate what you are doing. If you sell John Deere lawnmowers, you should own one. It would be like a stockbroker trying to sell you shares of a new stock. If he or she does not already own shares, should you really buy some? It would be pretty hard to convince someone to buy a DVD player when all you have at home is an old VCR. It only makes sense to own what you are selling.  By owning your product, you will be able to give a personal testimonial, which is a huge advantage over your competition.

An owner of a furniture store told me how his store sells mattresses for almost $400 over the national average selling price.  First let me start by telling you this store is in a city that has seen most of their major employers over the last three years either relocate or go out of business.  With most of the good paying jobs gone, his store has been able to overcome this obstacle by simply sleeping on their product.  That's right, the top two salespeople both have top quality, name brand mattress in their bedrooms at home.  Every time a consumer is looking at buying a new mattress, they make sure their customers lie down on the high-end models first.

Because the salespeople own the products they are selling, they are usually able to up sell their customers to the high-end models. They will sell the low-end models if it is what their customers want, but they make sure their clients know exactly what they are getting for their money. You will have a leg up on your competition if you believe in your products strongly enough to own them. Do not just own them because you receive an employee discount on them; own them because you believe in them.

If you are going to sell a product or service, you have to believe in it. You might be able to fool some consumers, but most will know if you are telling the truth. **If you believe, you will succeed**. A good test to see if you really believe in your product is to ask yourself one question. Would you hide from one of your past customers if you saw them out in public? If you would duck behind the nearest phone booth to avoid them, you have answered the question. If you would gladly walk up to them and say hello, you obviously are not worried about an unhappy customer. Do you think a salesperson who had sold you a crummy product, one that he or she knew you would not be satisfied with, would walk up to you and say hello? I don't think so. Someone who is only looking at his or her commission, and not looking out for their customers' best interest, will eventually fail, while a sales person who really cares about his or her customers will have a prosperous career. Most people generally live and work in the same community, and word travels fast if you are not a trustworthy person. Because of this, you need to treat your customers like you would treat your own Grandmother.

Not only do you need to believe in your products, you also need to know them inside and out. You should learn the differences between them to know how to match a consumer up with the right product. Remember though, product knowledge alone will not help you be a better salesperson. To be successful, you need to know more than just product information. Knowing your product is important, but knowing when to share this information with your customer is more important. Salespeople are sometimes so proud of what they know about their product, they want to explain every detail to their customer. Don't do this. Only give your customer enough information to answer their questions.

John worked for a company that distributed various home health care products. He recalled a sales meeting when the manufacturer of his water and air filtration systems asked if anyone had their products installed into their own homes? Only one person, John, raised his hand. I don't think it was a coincidence that he was also one of the company leaders in the sales of the systems. He believed in the products enough that he owned them. He also never let someone convince him that another product on the market was better than his. The day you let someone tell you that his or her product is better than yours, is the day you have lost your edge, and eventually you will start to believe that your products are inferior to your competition. Do not let this happen to you; because once you lose your belief in your products, your competition has won.

*Would you sell your Grandmother a product that you were not proud of or one that you would not buy for yourself?* You better not. Imagine how upset Granny would be if she found out you sold her something just to make a buck. She might not buy anything from you ever again and she would probably tell all of her friends. The same would be true if one of your clients found out you deceived them. Your Grandmother will trust you more if she knows you own what you are trying to sell her. You must believe you are selling the best product or service in your field, because there is a direct correlation between your belief in your product and your success. You need to own what you sell, and if you wouldn't own it, don't sell it. The only way to be proud of your products is to believe in them and own them. If you believe, you will succeed. Ask a group of salespeople to raise their hands if they own the products they sell. The salespeople with their hands up will be the most successful in the group. If it is not good enough for you, it sure isn't good enough for your Grandmother.

## Going the Extra Mile

A consumer is always going to take notice of a sales person who goes the extra mile. Or maybe I should say a salesperson willing to go an extra inch. Sometimes that is all it takes to separate yourself from your competition. A good example is Candice, who is a salesperson by day, and a chef by night. She enjoys her sales job, but she loves to cook. She is the type of person who would much rather cook you dinner at her home, than dine with you at the nicest restaurant in town. She sets herself apart from her competition and goes the extra mile by cooking for her clients. She occasionally will have her clients over to her home where she will prepare a full gourmet meal, which is a great way for her to get to know her customers on a personal level. After this relationship has been built, imagine how hard Candice's competition will have to work to take her clientele away. She has made it almost impossible for her competition to try and win over her clients' business. Not only does this solidify her business relationships, but she also gets to know her clients on a personal level. She has learned the best way to win her customer's heart is through their stomach.

You are probably thinking to yourself that you cannot cook a gourmet meal. That's okay. Most people do not cook like Candice. Of course she doesn't have every one of her clients over to her home for dinner. She would love to cook for all of them, but there are not enough days in the week. She only cooks for her larger clients that she wants to make a good impression with. For her smaller clients, she goes the extra mile a little differently. She cooks up her famous, secret salsa recipe and jars it. On each jar, she has her own special label with a personal thank you. Once she sells a client and the material is delivered, she personally delivers them a thank you basket complete with chips and a jar of her special salsa. Again, something her competition does not do. It takes effort to go the extra mile, and she definitely benefits from it. By building relationships that are almost impossible for her competition to compete with, she literally has her clients eating out of the palm of her hand.

During college, Mary worked as a manager in a pizza restaurant. For a while they had a marketing campaign called, *"No Problem."* Anything the customer requested, they would get. When they ordered their pizza, if they wanted avocados on it, it was *"No Problem."* Someone would drive to the grocery store, go to the produce section, buy an avocado, and the customer would get avocados on their pizza. If they wanted goat cheese instead of cheddar, again, *"No Problem."* By going the extra mile for their customers, it made them look a little better than their competition, and showed they were willing to go to great lengths to win over their customer's loyalty. The *"No Problem"* campaign was just their way of going the extra mile for their customers.

Another example of going the extra mile is Lee, who makes his living selling real estate, and also spends most of his leisure time fly-fishing on the river. His favorite time to fish is Monday through Friday, when most people are working, and he has yet to find someone in his favorite fishing hole during the week. For a guy who likes to spend workdays on the river, you would not think he would be the highest producer in his office. He is, and it is not hard to figure out why. When he is on the river, he is usually with one of his clients. It is a perfect way for him to mix business and pleasure. The relationships he has built with his clients while fishing are incredible. He does not get all of his clients on the river, but when he does, they seem to only want to buy and sell their property with him as their agent. He says he has the greatest job in the world, where he can *hook* a fish and *reel* in a customer, all in a days work.

Richard has been selling heavy equipment for sixteen years. As you can probably imagine, he has built up a large clientele. Over the last few years, he has played more golf than he ever thought possible. Sometimes playing up to four or five rounds in a week. With that being said, he is still the number one salesperson in his company. He has established his clientele over the years, and now closes most of his business on the golf course. This is just another example of someone who has gone the extra mile and benefited from it. You will hardly find him on the golf course without one of his clients. I would not, however, recommend this for a new salesperson just starting out their career. It takes time to build up your clientele, and Richard has worked very hard over the years to get to this point. He is just now reaping the rewards of his many years of hard work.

Jason has always done whatever it takes to keep his customers coming back, and he goes the extra mile for years after a sale. After the completion of every sale, he makes sure to find out the Birthday and Anniversary of each of his clients. He sells cars for a living and sometimes two or three years will pass before he gets repeat business from a previous client. Because of the amount of time between purchases, he came up with a simple method of staying in touch with them during the interim. He keeps each client's important dates written on 3x5 note cards, and files them in a note box sorted by month. Each month, he pulls out his cards and sends out greeting cards with a coupon for a free latte on Birthdays and a gift certificate for dinner on Anniversaries.

Yes, this does cost him some money, but the referral business has been incredible. Because he stays in constant contact with his past customers, he continues to get their repeat business as well as numerous referrals. He is constantly being sent new clients by referrals from his customers he sends cards to. Jason attributes much of his success to his Birthday and Anniversary program. Not a month goes by that he slacks off and forgets to send out his cards.

As his client list has grown, so has the time it takes to keep up with his program. Jason has since traded in his note box filled with cards for a computer program that stores and tracks his customers for him. Even though the information is stored differently, he still handwrites his cards instead of having his computer print them out for him. He will not allow innovation to take away from the personal touch he has tried so hard to maintain. The good news to his fellow salespeople is that his referral and repeat business keep him too busy to take walk-in customers. But year after year, his fellow salespeople watch Jason continue to out perform everyone at the dealership, maintaining his status as the top salesperson.

There is also another way to go the extra mile that will not cost you a dime. All it takes is a little effort. No matter what you say to one of your customers, **your actions will always speak louder than your words.** If your customer called you up to tell you they had just put a stain on their brand new carpet, what would you do? An average salesperson would probably ask them to drop by the store and pick up a carpet cleaning kit. A salesperson going the extra mile would ask their client when a convenient time would be to drop by their house. They would bring a cleaning kit and actually remove the stain for them. They would show their client the proper steps on cleaning carpet and leave them the kit at no charge for future spills.

Which salesperson left a bigger impression on their customer? If your customer called to ask you how to use their remote control for the new entertainment system you sold them, how would you handle the call? Again, the average salesperson would only try to explain it over the phone, and probably confuse their client even more than before they called. A salesperson going the extra mile would stop by their client's house after work, and personally demonstrate how to operate the system. Making a house call would leave a much better impression on your customer and will end up putting extra dollars back into your pocket by way of referrals.

Tammy has always tried to under promise and over deliver to her clients. After she has closed a sale, she usually gives her clients the worst-case scenario on the shipping. This is one way they will never be disappointed with her service. She might tell a customer that their product has to be special ordered, and delivery should be in approximately two weeks. This way if their order is ready to deliver in a week, they think she is a superstar. The last thing Tammy wants to do is to tell them a week, and have it take two. She would then have a disappointed customer. She also does what she says she is going to do. Don't you hate it when someone tells you they will call you with the information you have asked for, and the phone never rings?  If she tells a client she is going to do something, she does it.

It is the intangibles that separate the good salespeople from the bad.  If you are working the sales floor, and a consumer walks in the door 15 minutes before closing, are you going to treat them the same as a customer from three hours ago?  Chances are the consumer does not even realize the time, and has no idea when your store closes.  If you work with them regardless of the time, you will undoubtedly impress them once they realize the store is closed.  They will appreciate that you have gone the extra mile for them and will probably reward you for it.  If they ask if they are keeping you late, tell them you are there to serve them and it is not a problem.  This will be going the extra mile, big time. You have done something that most other salespeople would never do.  Most salespeople would tell a consumer their store is closing in 15 minutes the moment they walked in the door, immediately ending all chances of making a sale.

*How would you go the extra mile for your Grandmother?* It is the little things that will separate you from your competition and make you successful. If it looks like your Grandmother is worn out from shopping all day, you might offer her a chair and a cold drink. If she called to tell you she put a stain on her new sofa, why not go to your Grandmother's house and remove the stain for her? After all, you would not want your Granny to strain herself. It wouldn't cost you any money to go the extra mile for her, just a little effort. A little effort will go a long way towards your success, so always try to come up with something that will separate you from your competition. Whether you take your clients golfing or fishing, or send them Birthday or Anniversary cards, does not matter. It doesn't even matter if you spend any money on your clients, because the intangibles, like staying late with a client after closing, is also going the extra mile. Because there isn't enough time in the day to do all of these things, just find something to go the extra mile for your clients. No matter what you do, chances are it will pay for itself with the referral business alone. The next time you have a chance to do something extra for a client, imagine that he or she is your Grandmother, and go the extra mile.

## Closing the Sale

The process of closing a sale has changed over the last few years. In the past, salespeople would spend very little time in the introductory phase of the sale, and would start to show products before they even knew anything about their customer. More time was spent on trying to close the sale than anything else. Today, the most successful salespeople are the ones who make a connection with their clients before trying to sell them anything. Salespeople who try to use the old methods will probably chase a customer right out of their store. **Consumers want to feel like they know you, before**

**they will do business with you**. Like we discussed in chapter one, if you make a connection with your clients, you are miles ahead of your competition.

When you spend time getting to know your customers, your chances of closing a sale will increase dramatically. Always assume the sale and assume that you will get their business. Do not even think for a minute that they might shop somewhere else. It is amazing how far a little positive thinking will get you.

Take Matt, a sunglass salesman. He is an expert at assuming the sale. Now we are not talking the $5 sunglasses you buy at a booth set up on a street corner. Matt sells some of the finest sunglasses money can buy in a small store in San Diego, where his average pair of sunglasses retails for around $350. When a consumer walks into his store, he immediately greets them. Because most people wear sunglasses for an outdoor activity, he always asks if they participate in any sports. While some people say they ride bikes, go boating, or like to go camping, a lot of people just want to wear them to the beach, or while they are driving. Not only do his questions help him find out what his customers do for fun, but it also gets them to open up and talk about themselves.

He simply uses the *FORM method*, but only focuses on the **R**ecreation. Because Matt enjoys and participates in just about every outdoor activity, it enables him to have a real conversation with most of his customers. He has learned how to make a connection with his clients, and how to turn those connections into sales.

The most common mistake a salesperson will make in the closing phase of a sale is to not ask for the order. It seems so simple, but it happens all the time. Even though you have made a connection with your customer and up sold them into better products, there is still a fear of rejection when asking for the order. If you are new to sales, don't worry; you will learn to get over this fear. My definition of **success is running from failure to failure with a smile on your face**. You will never succeed in life without some failure and rejection along the way, and the only way to get rejected is by asking for the order, so do it. If you have done your job, this is just a formality, and is the only way for you to achieve success. Once you have taken the time to get to know your customer, and you have found out what they want to buy, asking for the order is the next logical step in the sale.

Different salespeople will tell you different ways they like to close a sale. Some might just write up the order and the sale just falls into place, while others might use one of the following: *"When would you like it delivered? ... How many would you like? ... When can we schedule the installation? ... Would you like me to see if we have one in stock? ... Which color did you want? ... Will that be cash or credit?"* These are all assumptive closes, the most common method of closing a sale, and are some of my personal favorites. Another method of closing, although not nearly as popular, is the direct approach. This is most effective when you have made a good connection with your customer and feel very comfortable with them. A direct close would be to simply ask for the order. Different closes work for different consumers, and most salespeople have two or three favorites they prefer. Find the ones that work for you and stick with them. Good closes are like good violins, the more you play them, and the better they will start to sound.

Learning how to handle objections is also an important part of closing. Kathy has been selling high-end cosmetics in a large department store for several years, and has been able to close a lot of business by learning to overcome objections. The most common objections she usually gets are: *"This makeup is so expensive compared to what I normally use. Does it actually work better than the regular store brands? Can I return it if I don't like the color?"* Kathy is able to handle these objections because she has planned ahead. She has made a list of every possible objection, and has gone over them until she is comfortable answering them. She has also done some role-playing with coworkers to make sure her responses are good enough to adequately answer any potential objection.

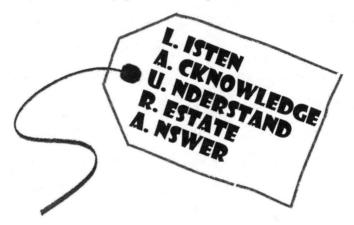

The best way to handle an objection is to plan ahead and role-play like Kathy has done. If you are trying to close a customer who has an objection, try to use the *LAURA* acronym. *Listen, Acknowledge, Understand, Restate, Answer. Listen* carefully to the objection so you clearly understand where your customer is coming from. *Acknowledge* the objection to make sure they know you are listening and that you are concerned. Make sure you *Understand* the objection. *Restate* the objection so your customer knows you heard them correctly. *Answer* the objection, and continue to close the sale.

While closing a sale, make sure to use whatever tools you have available. In-store financing and credit cards are great for making a sale less painful to your customer's pocketbook. With the dollar amount of a sale spread out over time, it makes it easier for a consumer to justify spending their money, and most consumers are willing to spend more if it means getting what they want. Today, almost all major purchases are paid for with credit. Reasons vary, but the fact is, people do use credit more often than cash. Air miles, reward points, and low interest promotions all help drive credit card sales.  Remember your competition is going to sell your customer on their financing offer if you don't.  Just be sure to offer all of your customers, all of your payment options, all of the time.

**If you were selling to your Grandmother, how would you close the sale?**  Closing your Grandmother's sale should be an easy task.  Don't make it difficult.  First off, make sure you ask for the order.  Do not let the fear of rejection stop you from making a sale.  Your Grandmother, as well as any consumer, is expecting you to ask for the order, so ask.  It might surprise you to find out how much business you would close if you would just ask for the order.  Also, by assuming your Grandma is only going to buy something from you should make it easier for you to ask.  *Keep it simple.*  She doesn't expect something for free and she definitely wants you to make a living, so give her your best price and she won't question it.  As long as you are giving her a fair deal, you should not have any trouble closing the sale.  The next time you are about to ask for an order, ask yourself if you would feel comfortable asking your Grandmother for the same order?  If it is good enough for your Granny, it is good enough for your customer.

Part II.

The Essentials

## Don't Limit Your Sales

I have met numerous salespeople who have limited their sales by simply being afraid to sell products that they cannot afford to buy for themselves. If you can only afford a $500 sofa, it does not mean your customer cannot afford to spend five times that amount. A few years ago, I wanted to purchase an entertainment center that was designed to go in the corner of a room. In one particular store, a salesperson told me that corner entertainment centers were very expensive, and were only available by special order. What? Did she say *very expensive?* I thought the customer was supposed to decide whether something is too expensive?  She acted like she did not even want to show them to me, and I almost had to twist her arm for her to show me a catalog of what was available.  Everything in the catalog was priced.  The prices were fine with me, but I guess it was a lot of money to her.  The amounts varied, but there were a few within my budget.  For a salesperson to do their job properly, they need to show all of their products, while trying to up sell their customers to better, more expensive items.  It was as if she had pulled the rug out from under her own feet.  What was she thinking?  Maybe she had prejudged me based on my appearance or my attire?  By prejudging me, did she think I could not afford to buy one?  Maybe they were too expensive for her budget?  I figured she must not have been in sales for very long, and she had not learned the basics of selling.  Even so, I was not about to give a commission to someone who did not understand this basic, fundamental selling principle.  She was limiting her sales by thinking her customer made the same amount of money as she did.  Always assume your customers make more than you do, lots more.

Alex has a very successful career selling cars at a luxury car dealership.  He has been selling ever since he graduated from college, even though he only intended to work in sales until he was able to find a job in marine biology. Eight years later, he is still selling for a living. He has, however, moved up from selling regular cars to selling luxury automobiles. His first six years were spent at a new and used Chevrolet dealership selling cars, trucks, and sport-utility vehicles. It was there where he learned how to have a successful career in selling and how you should **never limit your sales based on your own income**. He quickly discovered that his clients came from all backgrounds, some with money and some without, and he could not judge them by their looks alone. Just when he started to think someone couldn't afford a particular automobile, they would write out a check. Then when someone came in looking like a million bucks, they would end up having terrible credit. There was just no way to guess what someone could or could not afford based on their appearance.

Over half the vehicles on the lot were usually out of Alex's budget, but it did not stop him from selling them. He learned early in his career that just because he could not afford a particular automobile, did not mean his customer couldn't. He has made a nice living for himself and his family by selling cars.  Some of his clients, however, still make a lot more money than he does.

Because of his success in his first six years, he was promoted to his company's luxury car dealership and has now been selling Mercedes luxury vehicles for the last 2 years.  A lot of things have changed since moving up to selling more expensive automobiles, with the most noticeable being his paycheck.  Even though he makes a lot more money selling luxury, he has never forgotten what he learned in his early selling days.  He shows every vehicle on the lot, regardless of the sticker price.

Some of the cars are still out of his budget, but whether he can afford them or not does not matter.  He still shows every car on the lot to every consumer.  He knows he cannot limit his sales based on his own income, and to this day, it still surprises him to see which cars sell to which consumers. If he only sold the vehicles he could personally afford, his sales would certainly take a dramatic dive.

*Would you show your Grandmother all of your products even if you could not afford to buy them for yourself?* Don't limit your sales by only selling the items you can afford. Your Grandmother could have more money than you, so make sure to show her everything you have for sale. Just because you can't afford something, doesn't mean she can't. Consumers have their own wallets, and they might be thicker than yours. If you want to earn larger commission checks, don't limit your sales based on your own income. Make sure you show all of your products to every consumer, regardless of the price tag, because only your consumer knows what they can afford or what they are willing to spend. Remember, if you do not show your Grandmother the products that are out of your own personal price range, someone else will. Another salesperson might get your Grandma's sale, and the commission, because they did not limit their sales based on their own income.

## Keeping It Simple

It is important to keep your selling story simple. This does not mean, however, that you can fake your way through a sale. *Bull Shivitzing* will only get you so far. If you are going to sell something, you need to know your product. To be successful, you also need to know your competitions' products. This will help you to better explain your products' features and benefits compared to what your customer might be looking at across the street. In this chapter, we will discuss the importance of product information, as well as knowing when and how to use it in your selling.

Most new salespeople experience early success if they are not afraid to get their feet wet. Even if they don't know much about their product line, as long as they are willing to talk with consumers to find out what they are looking for, they will probably close a few sales. One of the reasons for this early success is actually by accident. Because a new salesperson is not usually completely comfortable with their new products, they tend to keep their sales presentation simple, and consumers are usually more receptive to a simple presentation versus a complicated one. A new salesperson does not always receive all the product training they should before working on the sales floor, and to avoid looking like a novice in front of their customers, they usually keep it simple.

A strange thing happens, however, when this same salesperson has been on the job for six months or so, and has had time to study up and learn about the different products that he or she is selling. You have probably heard the phrase, *"Enough information to be dangerous."* When salespeople get caught up in explaining all the details about their products, they sometimes forget about the basics. Consumers can easily get confused with all the features and benefits of the different products on the market, and more often than not, a confused consumer will walk out of a store empty handed. Pay attention to the buying signals your customer gives you and remember to **stop selling once you have sold your customer**. Most salespeople have their presentations down to a science, with a mental list of items to go through with each of their customers. If you only get halfway through your list, and your customer says *"yes"* or *"I'll take it,"* it is time to stop selling. You're done, so do not continue to try and sell what is already sold. If you don't stop, you stand a chance of your customer changing their mind, and if they walk out of your store without buying anything, you don't get paid. You cannot possibly sell every consumer you talk to, but it helps if you can keep your selling story simple and pay attention to your customer.

When you were brand new and didn't know very much about your product line, you kept it simple and were still able to close some sales. If you start overloading and confusing your customers, you have *hit the wall*. I define *"hitting the wall"* as a point in your selling career when closing a sale almost seems impossible. It is not a time to give up, but a time to look back to the past. If you *hit the wall*, you need to recognize it and quickly get over it. Don't get stuck. Remember what makes a salesperson successful.

*The wall* is a real problem for not only new salespeople, but it can also stop a veteran dead in their tracks. Depending on the salesperson, *the wall* can come as early as a month, six months, or even a year or two down the road. The main reason someone *hits the wall* is because they try to explain all the information they have learned about their products to every consumer during their presentations, and they forget to **keep it simple**.

Don't misunderstand me. I am not saying you shouldn't learn everything there is to know about your product. By all means, read every manual. Watch every video. Attend every seminar your company offers and learn everything you can. Product knowledge is extremely important. What I am saying is that you need to know when to use and when not to use this information. Some consumers are interested in every detail and others are just there to buy something. You need to know how to distinguish between each type of consumer.

My favorite analogy to use in sharing product information with your clients is a gunfight. In a gunfight, you only have so many bullets. The person you are shooting at, your customer, also has a limited number. Your product knowledge represents your bullets, and your customer's questions and objections are theirs. The key to winning a gunfight is to make sure you are not the first person to run out of bullets. Use them wisely. If your customer asks a question and fires off a bullet, make sure you only fire enough shots to answer their question. If you were selling cars, a consumer might ask about the engine under the hood of the car they are looking at. When you were brand new in the car business, you might have answered the question by simply replying, *"This car has a V6 engine and has plenty of power to cruise down the highway."*

Because you had only been selling cars for a short period of time, you answered the question with a simple answer. Each question your customer had, you responded by keeping it simple. They fired one bullet at you, and you fired one back. Most salespeople have great success using this method. Now let us go forward in time six months. You have now had time to go through your company sales training program. You have studied the warranty packages, and all the features of each make and model on the lot. You have been trained with *"enough information to be dangerous."*

Once again, you are showing a consumer a car when they ask about the engine under the hood. Six months ago this question was answered with a simple response. Now that you are a trained professional, your response to this question is much different. It is probably something like, *"Well, this car has a 4.7 liter, dual overhead cam, fuel injected V8 engine. It gets 14 miles per gallon in the city and 19 on the highway. The suspension is a high performance set up with anti-lock brakes and 20-inch wheels."*

I may have gone a little overboard, but I wanted to make a point. Remember how we talked about the key to winning a gunfight is to make sure you do not run out of bullets before your customer. Your customer shot off one bullet, and you countered by emptying both of your six-shooters. They still have a pistol full of bullets and you are empty, which means *you're dead.*

You lost the gunfight with your customer, as well as their sale. Chances are they are going to drive off your lot and go buy a car from someone else who isn't so complicated. Your customer asked a simple question, and you responded with a complicated answer. When you were brand new and didn't know much about cars, you were successful because you kept it simple. Now that you have completed your product training, you have made your selling too complicated. Remember, simple is always better than complicated.

This is what you call *hitting the wall.* I have talked to many salespeople who recall when they hit it, and most remember it as a difficult time in their selling career. Every salesperson has *hit the wall,* almost as if it's a right of passage into being successful. I want to try to help you avoid it altogether. As soon as you catch yourself talking too much about product information and complicating your presentations, grab your climbing gear, it is time to climb the wall. Go back to what made you successful in the beginning and keep it simple.

Robert sells 35mm cameras and is certainly one of the most knowledgeable people around on the subject. He knows things about cameras that few people would understand, including how they are designed to how the image is transposed onto the film. He has even been to a few of the manufacturing facilities to see them being assembled, and has talked to the people who work on the production lines. He has also met with researchers and developers of new innovations. I guess you could call him a walking encyclopedia when it comes to 35mm cameras.

Based on that, you might think that Robert is one heck of a salesman. I wish I could tell you he is. Do not misunderstand me; he sells a lot of cameras. Probably more than most, but he could sell even more if he would not get so technical with every consumer. I have seen him talk a consumer into a product, and then right back out of it. Because he gives them so much information, they sometimes start to second-guess their buying decision. All they wanted to know was if a new camera would take better pictures than their old one. Simple answers to questions and a demonstration is all that most consumers need from a salesperson. Do not complicate something that should be relatively simple.

There is even a noticeable difference between men and women consumers. Men tend to want more technical information when it comes to most things. Men want to know the horsepower, while women want to know if they can pass on the highway with ease. This is not always the rule, but fairly common. Speaking for myself, I have taken many things apart to see how they work. I don't, however, recall my wife taking apart the baby monitor when it stopped working to see if she could fix it. Some people just like technical information and some people don't. You need to be able to recognize when a consumer wants more than just a simple answer. You can usually read the expression on their face to see if your answer was sufficient. If you are not sure, just ask them if they want a more technical answer. Most people will probably say to keep it simple.

That's right. *Keep it simple.* Do not bore your customer with every piece of information about the product they are looking at. They probably don't care and probably wouldn't understand it anyway. Nothing is worse than a sales person who continues to pound a consumer over the head with all the features and benefits of their products, even after their eyes have started to glaze over. A consumer will get that frustrated and confused look in their eyes, and will look like they just want to fall asleep. As soon as they get the chance, they will leave your store and go find another sales person who is less confusing.

I am not saying to never give your customer technical information about the products they are looking at. Tell them whatever they want to know, but be careful not to overload and confuse them with too much technical garbage. It will make a consumer even more uncomfortable when you tell them something they don't understand. Besides, most of the technical information you learn about your products is actually meant for you, not your customers. The information is for you to know the differences between your products, so you can match a consumer up with the correct product. If a consumer asks how a surround sound stereo system works, they are not necessarily asking how the sound is transferred from the receiver to the speaker. They are probably asking how they put a DVD into a player and watch a movie in surround sound. Do you see the difference? They are asking a simple question. They fired a one-bullet question, so fire them a one-bullet answer. If they want a more technical explanation, they will ask for one. Just don't empty your guns unless you have to.

No two consumers are ever going to act alike. Sure there are similarities, but there are always going to be differences between them. One might require a lot more time and information, while another has already been educated on the product and knows exactly what they want. When you are working with a new customer, you need to **meet them at their level**. Find out where they are at so you know where you need to start. This means you must be prepared to help every level of consumer, from the expert to the novice. In doing so, you still need to keep it simple.

*Would you keep it simple if your Grandmother walked into your store?* Now let's suppose that your Grandmother is asking questions about the computers you are selling. How are you going to treat her? If she asks you which kind of computer she needs to buy to be able to send e-mail, what are you going to tell her? I'm sure you are not going to bore her with all the details of the different kinds of computers she could buy. You won't tell her about the size of the hard drive or the speed of the processor. You are going to show her a computer system that will allow her to send e-mail and print pictures of her grand kids. You are going to *keep it simple*. Sure, you could go through all the computer information you know, but it won't impress your Grandmother. The only person who will be impressed with your level of product knowledge is probably yourself. It will only confuse her and make things worse. If your Grandmother happens to be a little more computer savvy than most other Granny's out there, and wants to know about picture editing software, than show her. Just remember to only fire as many bullets as it takes to answer her questions. Imagine your next customer is your Grandmother. How will you keep it simple?

# Attitude

A positive attitude is essential in every part of your life, including sales. You must have your game face on at all times. No matter what is happening in your personal life, you cannot let it get in the way of your selling. When a consumer first walks into your store, you need to greet them with a smile. If you just found out that your car needs $500 worth of engine work, or if your spouse just called to tell you that the washer and dryer stopped working, you can't let it show. This is life, and life is going to happen to everyone. Things are never going to be perfect at home and in your personal life, and how you deal with these issues will determine your success. Your customer does not want to hear about your problems. Remember, they have their own problems too. When you are in sales, your game face is a nice smile and a pleasant voice. You will be amazed to see how these two little things can start an introduction off in the right direction.

A number of salespeople have trouble with this simple concept. What is so hard to understand? A consumer who is shopping does not care if your house just needed a new roof. They really don't. You may think they care, and you may want to tell them about it, but they really do not want to know. A salesperson might ask a consumer how they are today, and they will probably get a response similar to, *"Fine, how are you?"* Your customer is not really asking you how you are. This is just a natural response to your question. Believe it or not, some salespeople will actually start explaining to their customer that their dog just died, their car is broke down, and other things as if they really wanted to know. This is not a good way to make a connection with your new customer. You need to have a positive attitude and stay professional. They came into your store to look at your products. They have probably been shopping all day and have been to multiple stores and talked to numerous salespeople. If you are not positive and do not look happy to be there, remember, **there are other stores**

**and other salespeople your customer can choose to do business with**. A smile is contagious and will take you a long way towards success. If you seem unhappy, you stand a good chance of losing your customer to your competition.

One of the best things a coworker can ever say to you is, *"You always have a smile on your face and you never seem to have a bad day. How do you do it?"* This is a nice compliment. Everyone has bad days, no matter who they are. Some people, however, do a better job separating their personal life from their work life. If you have not had anyone ever say this to you, it is not necessarily a bad thing, but you need to ask yourself if your line between work and home has become blurry. Office politics and gossip are a part of any job, and are almost impossible to avoid. Make sure, however, when you step out of the office and onto the sales floor, you leave your problems behind.

I worked with a sales person who had this very problem. Sarah was one of those people that could put a damper on just about everything. Nothing in her life seemed to go right. Lucky me, I had to share an office with her, and it wasn't easy to listen to her talk about all of her problems on a daily basis. I have just always believed that life is what you make of it, and if you think you are happy, than you will be happy. People who are negative tend to have an unhappy life, and Sarah was just one of those people. It was hard to believe some of the things she would actually say to her customers. She would tell her clients all about her personal problems whenever they were willing to listen.

Now there is a time and a place to talk about these things, and during a sales presentation is definitely the wrong time. A consumer is in your store to buy something, not to listen to someone else's problems. Sarah would talk to anyone who would listen to her, and it probably will not surprise you to hear that she was terrible in sales. If she could have just learned to put a smile on her face when a consumer walked in the door, she would have been a lot more successful. Instead, she scared away most of her customers and eventually had to move onto another career. Do not let negative events in your life affect your sales the way Sarah did. Remember everyone has problems, and the last thing they want to hear about is yours.

Having a bad attitude is detrimental to your ability to sell. There is no reason to ever put up an attitude towards a consumer. No matter what they might have said or done, to give a client some attitude will only make things worse. Don't forget there are lots of other salespeople your customer can do business with. Max had been selling mountain bikes for quite a few years, and felt strongly about his products. Early in his career, he was working with a consumer who was new to biking and was not very knowledgeable on the subject.

When Max steered him into his favorite brand of bicycle, his customer immediately said of all the available brands, this was the one brand he would never buy. Max knew his customer did not know what he was talking about, because in all the years he had sold bikes, this was the only brand he rarely had problems with. The customer explained that he had a friend who was unhappy with one he had bought, so he wanted to avoid them altogether. Max immediately developed an attitude towards his customer, and felt his customer was an idiot for believing his friend. He made it obvious to him that he felt this way. Not the smartest thing to do when you are trying to win your customer's business. His customer felt his attitude, and Max lost any chance of making a sale. His customer walked out the door empty handed, undoubtedly heading to one of his competitors.

What good did it do for Max to give his customer some attitude? Did he think he could talk his customer out of buying a new bicycle just because he didn't want to buy a certain brand? Not likely. His customer walked out the door and probably did business with another store. A good salesperson would have just showed their customer another brand, and closed the sale. Max could have easily done that, but he didn't. He gave him attitude and wanted his customer to know that he was more knowledgeable, and lost the sale in the process. This was a mistake he only made a few times early in his career before realizing he was only hurting himself. Even though he strongly believes in one particular brand of mountain bike, he still sells a few other brands that are of similar quality. They are not his personal favorites, but he cannot always sell his favorite brand. He learned from his early mistakes, and today he never lets his attitude or personal feelings get in the way of making a sale.

Nathan, who has sold furniture for over 20 years, had an experience with a customer he has never forgotten. His store had large windows that lined the front of the building, which was a nice feature to have on a sales floor. You could always see every time someone either walked in or out of the store. One day he was in the rear of the store helping an older woman. While he was showing her new table lamps, he happened to be looking out the front windows while talking to her. Nathan stood roughly six foot tall, and his customer couldn't have been much taller than four feet. When she noticed he was not looking her in the eye, she angrily said, *"Young man, I realize my little sale may not be very important to you, so if you have another customer you would rather be helping, go right ahead. I don't appreciate you talking down to me and treating me like I'm unimportant."*

Nathan felt terrible. He did not have another customer to help. In fact, she was the only customer in the store. He realized he must have upset her because he was not looking at her while he was addressing her. Granted, he was over two feet taller than her, but nonetheless, he should have made better eye contact with her. Years later, he always makes sure to maintain eye contact with each of his clients. He does not stare them down, but he makes sure to look them in the eye when he is speaking with them.

*If your Grandmother walked into your store, would you have a good attitude?* If you didn't already have a smile on your face, you should have one now. You do not want your Grandmother to know that you are having a bad day. Even though you may want to tell her you got a flat tire on the way to work, you won't. You want her to be in the best possible mood while shopping in your store. For Grandma to open her checkbook and give you money, she needs to be happy. If she is depressed because you just told her your dog died, you will probably lose the sale. Don't do or say anything to put a damper on your customers' spirits. Unhappy people generally don't spend money. They came into your store to buy something, so keep them in the buying mood with a good attitude. Besides, why would anyone want to put his or her Grandmother in a bad mood?

## Moment of Truth

The moment of truth can happen at any time during a sale. This is the point when you can either make or break it. Veteran sales people, who know their competitors' products, as well or better than their own products, look forward to this. This is put up or shut up time and a good example of this is a hardwood flooring salesperson. After a consumer has shopped all over town, chances are they are pretty confused. They have probably talked to three or four different salespeople who have all had a different story to tell about each product. *"This wood floor is the best value for your dollar ... this brand has the best finish ...this is our special sale item ... this is made by the best manufacturer ... this one has the best warranty ... this floor won't scratch."*

When a consumer has shopped all over town, what they are probably still shopping for is a salesperson worthy of giving their business to.  Do not forget that a consumer is not only shopping for a product, but also a salesperson to do business with.  They are looking for someone who is knowledgeable, trustworthy and someone who will take care of them in the event of a problem.  This is where the moment of truth comes in.  Every salesperson seems to have a different story to tell about the products they sell.  Some even have different stories about the same products, so it is no wonder a consumer can get so confused.  Some salespeople will say anything to get a sale, including stretching the truth or telling a downright lie.

Steve walked into a flooring store with a sample in hand of a cherry hardwood from a competitor down the street.  Both stores sold the same product, and he wanted to compare their prices.  As he talked to a salesperson, he told her he wanted to buy this floor because another salesperson had told him this particular brand would not scratch.  Steve was told it was the strongest, most durable product on the market. Here is where a veteran salesperson can grab a hold of a sale and take it straight to the bank.

Remember that Steve is shopping for two things, a hardwood floor and a salesperson. If a consumer has been told something about a product they are looking to purchase that is false or incorrect, you need to inform them. In this case, Steve believes this particular hardwood floor will not scratch. If you know this is not true, you are making a mistake if you choose not to tell your customer. If a consumer has unreal expectations about your product, it is your job to tell them the truth. In most cases, they will be happy you did. A veteran salesperson would probably tell Steve something like, *"All the years I have been selling*

*hardwood flooring, I have yet to find one that does not scratch and dent. As a consumer, you have a choice to do business with whomever you choose. It's up to you. If you believe the person who told you it wouldn't scratch, get it in writing, and buy it from them."*

If you know you are telling the truth and being honest about your product, you have nothing to worry about. That is why this point of the sale is called the *moment of truth*. You will either lose the sale, or you will have a customer who appreciates your honesty and is ready to do business with you. If you lose them to your competition, it is okay. If their floor doesn't look good in a year, they will hopefully remember what you told them, and you will get their future business. Most consumers appreciate a sales person who won't give them a song and dance. They want accurate information so they can make an educated buying decision, based on facts, not fiction.

Take another example of a guy who has sold computers for the last seven years. Bryan was the kid that everyone always came to when they had problems with their computer. Some people just seem to understand those crazy machines, and he knew them like the back of his hand.

When he first started selling computers, he spent his first two years working at a large electronics retailer. He was always amazed at how many people buying computers did not really know what they were actually buying. Consumers relied on the expertise of the salespeople to determine which type of computer they should buy, and more often than not, consumers would buy a machine that did not meet their requirements. Consumers would sometimes purchase systems that were bigger and faster than anything they ever needed. Even worse, sometimes they would find out the machine they bought was not big or fast enough to properly run their software.

He watched how consumers were dissatisfied with their purchases on a regular basis. Even though a consumer would tell their salesperson exactly what they wanted, they would not always get what they asked for. With as fast as the computer industry changes, most equipment cannot be returned after 30 days. With the high employee turnover at large electronics dealers, a customer would have a hard time blaming their salesperson, since chances were good that they no longer worked there. After two years, there came a point when he could not take it anymore and he needed to make a change.

Bryan decided to go to work for a smaller, locally owned company that specialized in computers, where he has now been in professional computer sales for the last five years. Here is an example of when Bryan had to use the *moment of truth* with a potential customer. A consumer came in one day looking for a computer system he would be able to efficiently operate his small business with. He wanted to use the system for every aspect of his business, including invoicing, payroll, accounts receivable, accounts payable, and advertising. This consumer had shopped all over town before he walked into Bryan's store. Bryan showed his customer exactly what he needed to buy and how much it was going to cost for the system to work to his satisfaction.

His price was the highest out of all the other stores his customer had shopped so far. He explained to his customer that in order to meet his expectations, everything on his proposal would need to be purchased. His customer did not want to buy the entire package, and thought Bryan was just trying to sell him unneeded hardware and software. He told his customer if he did not want to buy the entire package, then he didn't want to sell him anything. Yes, Bryan was about to walk away from a potential $6,000 order. He felt strongly about his reputation and he was willing to walk away from an order, large or small, to avoid a problem and an unhappy customer. This was the *moment of truth.*

Bryan knew that if he sold an incomplete computer system to a consumer, it would come back to haunt him, and the word-of-mouth advertising would be hard to overcome. His company had a reputation of the highest quality and highest level of service in town. He knew that if this consumer bought an incomplete system from his competition, the word-of-mouth advertising would actually help him in the long run. Bryan was willing to walk away from a sale to prove it. He knew when the system failed as he predicted, he would have this consumer begging him for help. Once that happened, he would have a **customer for life**, which would be worth much more than the profit of a $6,000 sale that was undoubtedly going to have problems.

About to walk away from a sale, it was obvious that Bryan plans on being in computer sales for a long time. If he were only worried about his commission, he would not have cared whether the system would have worked properly or not. He would have just sold the job to make his commission. He understands the value of a customer over their lifetime versus a one-time customer, and he would much rather have a *customer for life*.

The best way to tell if a salesperson plans to be around for a while is to see whether he or she would sell something, even though a consumer has unreal expectations about the product or service. You might already know if you plan on making a career out of your current sales job. If you plan on being successful, remember that it is okay to walk away from a potential problem. If you know you will be working at your same job for the next five to ten years, don't worry about it, your customer will be back. They will remember the fact that you told them you have too much integrity to sell them a product that will not perform to their satisfaction. If you don't plan on staying at your job, you are probably one of those salespeople who would sell anything, knowing full well it will not meet your consumer's expectations. You would not really care since you are not going to be around when they come back to the store to complain. Most storeowners would agree that it is much easier to avoid a problem than to deal with one, so don't sell a product that will not perform to your customer's expectations.

It has always amazed me what some salespeople are willing to say and do to get a sale. My mom always taught me that the best way to not get caught in a lie was to simply not tell one.  **If you tell the truth, you don't have to remember what you said**.  It is easier than telling a lie, and you just have to remember what *actually* happened instead of what you *said* happened.  I have met some pretty good storytellers in my life, and I can usually spot them fairly quickly.  Most consumers can spot a storyteller as well.

If you are in sales, you do not want to be a liar.  If your customer feels like you are lying to them or not being upfront with them, they will probably take their business elsewhere.  Trust is extremely important.  If you have a *moment of truth* in a sale, you need to tell the truth, or you lose.  Remember too that the Internet provides people with a lot of information from a wide variety of sources, and there is a good chance your customer might already know the correct answer before they even ask a question.  They could be testing you to see if you are being honest or if you know what you are talking about.  If you do not know the answer, you should respond by simply saying, *"I don't know ... let me find out."*  Don't forget you are selling yourself, as well as your product, and if you do not know the answer to a question, your best response is always an honest one.

*If your Grandmother walked into your store, would you tell her the truth?* When you were a kid, do you think your Grandmother knew when you were telling her a story? She probably not only knew when you were lying, but she knew it before you even opened your mouth. If you imagine that your customer is your Grandmother, you would probably tell the truth, the whole truth, and nothing but the truth. You wouldn't even chance it. Do you know anyone who could pull one over on his or her Grandmother? I can't stand finding out I was lied to, and neither can your consumers. The point here is simple, just tell the truth and you will stay out of trouble. Don't make up a crazy story to sound good in front of your customer. Make sure your story is the truth, and don't be afraid to tell it. The moment of truth is a good thing for an honest salesperson. As long as you have your customer's best interest at heart, don't worry. Like Grandmothers, most consumers are able to separate fact from fiction. If you lie to your customers, the only truth will be that your competition will win over your customer and their business.

## Reading Body Language

An important key to your success is learning how to read body language. It is essential for you to know how to read a consumer and know how to interact with them. If you are taking a customer through the features and benefits of a product, you need to make sure they understand what you are saying and that you do not lose them. If you notice their eyes glazing over, you have probably confused them, and you should back up and find where you lost them. You must pay attention to the body language of your customers to know when they want something or to know when to back off. If you do not watch for these signs, you stand a good chance of rubbing your customer the wrong way and upsetting them.

I had an experience that made me realize some people either don't know how to read body language, or don't pay attention to it. Below is an example of when a person failed to watch the body language of their customer, and in turn, they did not know when **too much service was bad service**.

My family and I decided to go out to dinner at a fancy burger restaurant. We walked in the door and were greeted by a host who asked us if we needed anything or required any special services. We said we were fine, and selected a table off to the back of the restaurant near the video games to keep my son entertained during dinner. We walked up to the front counter to place our order, and when we came back to the table, the host was waiting to make sure we were still doing okay. Again we said we were fine, so we helped ourselves to our drinks. While my son and I played video games, the host had again asked my wife and my mother if they needed anything. At this point, my wife was getting more and more irritated with the host. It was not like she was making eye contact with him or giving him signals like she needed something. He just kept pestering us by checking back every few minutes to see if we were still doing okay.

Dinner was finally ready, so we all walked over to get our plates to dress our burgers at the condiment counter. Again, the host was right there to see if we needed anything! At this point, I told him we had been here dozens of times, and we really didn't need any assistance. We all sat down to eat dinner. While eating, he came by three more times to make sure everything was okay. We were so annoyed by him that we hardly enjoyed our dinner. I felt like he just did not get the point that we were fine and did not require any assistance. We finally had to be rude for him to get the message to stay away from our table. None of us could believe he did not realize how he was annoying us. He just didn't get it. Finally, we were done with our meal and could hardly wait to leave. The host was driving us all crazy.

Before we left, we thought someone should know how obnoxious the host had been so they could correct the problem. Because this was our favorite place to have a good burger, we wanted the manager to know that our dining experience was far from enjoyable. We had eaten there more times than we could count, and this was our first bad experience. I walked up to the manager and asked if I could talk to her about her host on duty this evening. I explained to her how he had come up to our table more than a dozen times, and with a blank look on her face, she replied, *"Sir... I'm not sure where you're from, but that is what we call good service."*

I could not believe my ears. I was the paying customer and she was telling me what good service was. I tried to explain to her that I had worked for a number of years in the restaurant business, and I definitely knew the difference between good and bad service. Checking on a table a dozen times during a meal was the furthest thing from good service. If this is what we have to look forward to on our next visit, we will not be back. To my dismay, she said she was sorry I felt that way and looked at me as if I were an idiot.

Now if you are thinking to yourself that the host was not a salesperson, you're wrong. He might not have sold us our dinner, but he was there to sell us the service of the restaurant. This is just an example of a sales person who did not recognize or register our body language. He obviously did not see how aggravated we had all become over the course of our dinner, and as a result, we have not been back since. Some people just do not know when *too much service is bad service*.

Most salespeople have good intentions when it comes to giving good service to their customers. Sometimes too much of this good service can backfire and become bad service. Take the earlier story about Jason, the sales person who goes the extra mile by sending his clients Birthday and

Anniversary cards to stay in contact with them between purchases. One reason his program is successful for him is because he personally writes out each card and sends them himself. He does not let someone else write them out for him. It may sound unimportant, but the fact that he personally sends each card shows his clients he genuinely cares about them. People know the difference between a piece of mail from a mailing list versus an actual handwritten note or card.

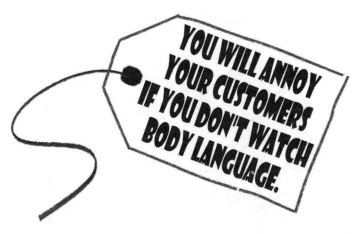

Everyone has probably received at least one card from someone they have done business with. Most of the time, it is usually preprinted, and is not actually signed by anyone. Let's not forget that consumers are not stupid and know when they are receiving personalized service. It is always humorous to get one of these cards from a company you have not done business with in the last five years.

Receiving one of these cards is a good example of how something that has good intentions, backfires. It shows how some people just add your name to a database and treat you like a number instead of a real person. A sales person who treats their clients like they would treat their own Grandmother will be more successful than someone who does not.

*If your Grandmother walked into your store, how would you read her body language?* It is important to watch for the different expressions on your Grandmother's face while she is shopping in your store. If you are explaining the features and benefits of a product, her face is a good indicator to see if she understands what you are saying. If her eyes are glazing over, you may have confused her. If you don't go back and find where you lost her, Granny will probably get irritated, and chances are she won't buy what you are trying to sell her. Facial expressions, posture, and the tone of a persons' voice are all types of body language that a salesperson needs to pay attention to. You should always be watching for these silent signals to know if your customer is with you or not. Picture your Grandmother's face when she caught you sneaking a cookie from her cookie jar. Now think of that face as a reminder to never forget to pay attention to your customer's body language.

## Fixing Problems is Your Time to Shine

Sometimes things go wrong with the products we sell. Don't let a problem get you down. Nothing ever seems to go exactly the way we hope it will. If you sell things like clothing, electronics, or merchandise a consumer can carry out of your store, you probably have few problems. Listen up though, in case something does happen to go wrong. If you sell things like cars, appliances, furniture, flooring, or other products that are usually delivered or installed, you will probably encounter a problem every now and again. How you handle a problem is more critical than the problem itself.

Know that problems will happen, and learn to look forward to them and embrace them. Put yourself in your customers' shoes and imagine how they must feel. How would you want someone to fix the problem if it was yours? Always remember that fixing problems is your time to shine.

A few years ago, I had purchased a new computer for my job as a sales rep. Traveling every week on the road makes owning a laptop a must. The computer I replaced had served its purpose, and was a lot slower than the current models available. I did not have any brand loyalty or a store that I preferred, so I bought a computer that fit my needs, at the price I wanted to pay. If you have ever bought a new computer, you know it takes a while to get your software set up the way you like it, and this was no exception. Once all my software and documents were loaded, I was back in business. Everything was fine for the first three months, and then the problems began.

I had sent in my computer three different times to an out of state service center because of the problems I was experiencing. Lucky me, each time the repairs took a week, and it had really started to cause me headaches by not having my portable office. And of course, each time they sent it back to me, the problems were not corrected. I finally decided to take the computer back to the store where I had purchased it. I had hoped the store manager would put an end to my entire ordeal. He listened to my frustrations, and after checking my paperwork, he decided I had been through enough hassle, and he asked me to select a new computer in exchange for my problem stricken unit. My problem had been solved. Even though his store policy was no returns after 30 days, he did it anyway. Why? Because he felt it was the right thing to do.

Before this process, I had no store loyalty when it came to buying a computer. Not any more. I will definitely buy my next computer from the same store. Had I not encountered any problems with it, I would have probably bought my next computer somewhere else. I would have shopped for the best price and then made my purchase accordingly. By having a problem, they have gained a future customer. This is an example of how someone took care of a problem in exchange for a customer for life. Now I am not saying that problems are good, but when they do occur, how you handle them can make all the difference in the world.

PROBLEMS TO SOLVE ARE NOTHING MORE THAN AN OPPORTUNITY TO EXCELL.

Jake had a problem that had been getting worse by the day. He had been waiting a long time to throw a Super Bowl party at his house. His wife told him for years, the only way she would let him have one was if his favorite team made it to the big game. After 12 years of marriage, that day was about to come true. All season, his team was playing extremely well, and by November he started making the preliminary arrangements for the Super Bowl party. A group of about thirty friends and family gathered each year for the big event. Each year the party was held at a different house, and this was finally Jake's year. He thought a great way to put his wife into the football spirit was to buy her all new furniture for her house. They had not bought new furniture since they were first married, and after 12 years, what better occasion than a Super Bowl party. They shopped around until finally deciding on a beautiful living room set, and a new big screen television. They were excited about having everyone over to their home and they wanted it to look good.

Everything was going great. Jake's team won all their games in December, and the playoffs looked like a breeze. With a first round bye, they won two games and were headed straight to the Super Bowl. Only one problem, the living room set Jake and his wife had special ordered for the big day was not going to be ready for delivery until a week after the game. This was not good, and had Jake pretty upset with Mike, his salesperson. The set was originally supposed to be delivered by Christmas, then by New Years. Each week the delivery date was pushed back another week. With the end of January approaching rapidly, something had to be done.

The tension between Jake and Mike had been building and was about to blow. Jake just wanted his furniture, but Mike couldn't deliver what he didn't have. The last thing Jake wanted to see would be all of his friends and family sitting on the floor during the game.

Finally, Mike was able to come up with a resolution to fix the problem. He offered to have Jake and his wife come back into the store to have them pick out anything they wanted, and the store would loan it to them until their furniture was ready to be delivered. He wanted their new living room set for the party, and he had it, sort of. It was not exactly what they ordered, but it took care of their problem. The party went off without a hitch, including his team winning the championship trophy. A week after the game, the store finally delivered their new furniture and took back the pieces they gave them on loan. If the sale had gone without a hitch, the salesperson would not have had the chance to fix a problem. Who knows how much referral business Jake would have sent to his salesperson if the sale had been flawless. By taking a problem and turning it into a positive situation, Mike left a good impression on his customer. Most consumers will not hold a problem against their salesperson if it was out of their control. They will, however, hold them responsible if they handle the problem poorly, or without sympathy.

*If your Grandmother walked into your store with a problem, how would you fix it?* You should try to keep your Grandmother as happy as possible if she encounters a problem. They are never any fun, but problems do give you an opportunity to excel and to show your customer just how good you really are at your job. If your Grandmother has a problem, take care of it quickly and painlessly. If she is having engine trouble with the new car she just purchased from you, make sure she gets your best loaner car until hers is fixed. If your customer were your Grandmother, how would you accommodate her? When you have a problem, try to find a way to make it a positive for both you and your customer. When you fix a problem, and make your customer happy, they will probably remember you more than if they didn't have a problem in the first place. Because problems are going to happen, you might as well embrace them, and fix them as if your customer were your own Grandmother.

## *Shopping for the Whole Package*

When a consumer is shopping for a product or service, they are not just shopping for something to buy. They are also shopping for a salesperson to do business with. In essence, they are shopping for the whole package. You might be a salesperson at the biggest appliance dealer, with the largest selection and the best prices in town. This will, however, not guarantee your success. Do not forget that your customers are shopping for more than just product, price, service, and selection. They are also shopping for someone to give their business to. More to the point, they are looking for someone to give a commission check to. As a salesperson, be aware that your customer is looking at more than just your products and services. They are also looking at you.

If this is the case, what can you do to increase your sales? What can you do to separate yourself from your competition? Again, just like how easy it is to show a genuine interest in the sale, separating yourself from your competition is not very difficult. Most of the basics actually take place before you leave your house for work. It all starts with a nice hot shower. Deodorants, hair spray, razors, and makeup all help, and believe it or not, these things are not standard procedure for all people. Like it or not, we live in a society that prefers a clean cut, clean shaven, nicely dressed, well maintained, nice smelling person. Earlier we talked a lot about prejudging. Do yourself a favor and don't give consumers a reason to prejudge you based on your own appearance.

When you are trying to make a good first impression, if you open your mouth and have bad breath, you are in trouble. If you still have part of your breakfast bagel stuck in your teeth, your customer is not going to hear a word you are saying. Speaking of your teeth, it is important to have a nice smile. **Smiles are contagious, and are an inexpensive way to improve your looks**. When I was younger, I went through five years of misery with braces on my teeth. Back then I was too young to understand how much a nice smile and nice teeth would mean to me when I was older. When you are in sales, a nice smile is definitely worth a million bucks. Any money you spend at the dentist is money well spent, and a wise investment in your future.

Clothes are also very important, but it is not always how much you pay for them or the name brand that matters. What matters is how you take care of them and how well they look on you. You can have on a $50 dress shirt with an $80 tie, and if your shirt is not ironed, your customer will only see your wrinkled shirt. Your appearance tells a consumer what kind of person you are without saying a word. They sure won't be very excited to give you their business if it looks like you do not care about your own appearance, or you look like a slob. If your pants look like you are waiting for a flood, don't wear them. If your dress shoes look like you just stepped in a mud puddle, get them shined. It is also important to stay in style. My wife is always going through my closet and removing things that she will not let me wear anymore. Imagine seeing a salesman wearing a brown polyester suit. How fast would you run? Your customer is shopping for the whole package and part of your success will be determined by how well your package looks. If you want to have a successful career in selling, make sure you are in style, and that you look, feel, and smell good. If a consumer had a choice between two different salespeople, they would undoubtedly choose the more successful looking of the two.

Because a consumer is looking at more than just products and services when they are shopping, the salesperson is always a part of the equation. This is why some salespeople can be successful, regardless of the quality of their product line. It is a big advantage over your competition if you look good. If a salesperson comes across as a shyster, it does not matter how good his or her products are. Most consumers will not do business with someone they don't trust. When making their purchase, they might as well be making out the check directly to the salesperson. After all, it is the salesperson they are doing business with. Sure the store is important, but not nearly as important as its salespeople.　Without them, the store would be out of business.

**If your Grandmother walked into your store, would she buy from you?**　You would not show up at your Grandmother's house looking like you had been out all night and didn't have time for a shower. You also wouldn't have food in your teeth or coffee breath. Not a chance. You would make sure your hair was nice, your clothes were clean, and your teeth were brushed. The next time you are going to work, look in the mirror. Ask yourself if you saw your Grandmother today, would she be proud of her Grandson or Granddaughter? If the answer is yes, than get on the sales floor and set a new sales record. If the answer is no, get your act together. **If you look successful, you will feel successful, and if you feel successful, you will be successful**. Make sure to keep your act clean, so you can clean up on your competition. Just like when you were a kid, you should always try to make your Grandmother proud.

## Referrals

The most important key to being a successful salesperson is getting referrals. Your success and your paycheck both depend on them. The sales people who figure this out early in their career are the men and women who live in big homes, drive nice cars, and live happily ever after. In order to receive referrals from your clients, you will need to apply something from each of the previous chapters to your selling technique. Referrals are what divide the top salespeople from the average ones, because the top salespeople always get referrals. One salesperson told me you have not really closed a sale until you get a referral from the original sale. Only then is a sale complete.

To better understand referrals, try to imagine a sale from your client's point-of-view. John and Stephenie walked into a flooring store to buy new flooring for their home of ten years. They plan on living out their days in this home and they want to update it with style. Lets take a look at how two different salespeople handle the same situation.

Bill, a brand new salesman, takes the easy road. He walks John and Stephenie over to the in-stock specials. When these don't catch their eye, he starts to show them the different options that can be special ordered. He starts by showing them the least expensive items and works his way up. With little excitement, he convinces them on purchasing carpet and vinyl for their whole house. The materials are installed three weeks later, just in time for Stephenie's monthly bridge party. She is excited to see how her friends will react to her new carpeting in her entire home and all the new vinyl in the kitchen and bathrooms. The party comes and goes with only one woman even noticing that she had bought new flooring. As you can imagine, Stephenie was disappointed and confused as to why no one had said anything.

So what's the problem? When they decided to remodel their home, was it not for their own pleasure and enjoyment? It wasn't for their friends? Wrong! People love getting compliments on their homes, and John and Stephenie were no exception. It had taken a lot of years to save enough money for their purchase, and only one friend had even noticed. Why didn't more of her friends notice she had all new flooring throughout her house?

Now let us look at the same scenario, but this time with a different sales person who has been selling flooring for the last 12 years. Brenda greets her new customers as they walk into her store. She immediately asks about the project at hand and is visibly excited about helping John and Stephenie turn their house into their dream home. After 12 years in the business, she knows how important it is to show her clients that she cares about their project. She takes the time to find out exactly what they are trying to accomplish by investing in their home.

A consumer might be fixing up their house to sell, which means they are probably trying to spend as little money as possible for the highest return on their investment. Most consumers, however, are looking to turn their house into their home, and are willing to spend the money to do it. These are the type of clients that Brenda prefers to work with. She starts off by showing John and Stephenie the top of the line flooring first, before showing them less expensive items. She knows the nicer their home turns out, the happier they will be, and the more likely they will tell their friends where they made their purchase. Brenda helps them decide on a thick, plush carpet for the living room, hallway, and bedrooms.

After showing them all of their options for the kitchen and bathrooms, they end up deciding on hardwood for the kitchen and ceramic tile for both baths. They even decide on a floral printed carpet for the fine dining room. Three weeks later, the materials are installed into their home just in time for Stephenie's monthly bridge party. As her friends start showing up, they immediately notice all the new flooring. They absolutely love the hardwood, tile, and especially the floral print in the fine dining room. Over half of the women ask her where she bought her new flooring, and without hesitation, she tells them to go see Brenda. She lets them know how she was so helpful and wonderful to work with from beginning to end. Stephenie finally had her dream home and she loved every bit of the attention she received from all of her friends.

The difference between doing business with one salesperson versus another can sometimes be profound. A rookie mistake is to think that simply selling a customer and getting the job is the goal. The same consumer goes into the same store and two different salespeople ended up with two different results. The veteran salesperson has a happy customer while the rookie has an unhappy one. Bill not only hurt himself, but he hurt his store's reputation as well. Remember, he sold the least expensive carpet he could in order to get the job and his commission. This is short-term thinking. If Bill wants to stay in this business long-term, he needs to understand the value of referrals. This will also hurt the store down the road, because an unhappy customer will always remember not to shop at this store ever again. The goal is to have a happy, satisfied customer, and to have them refer others to you. By just trying to collect a commission, a salesperson is not looking at the big picture, and is missing the boat.

Now Brenda, the veteran, showed why she is so successful in the flooring business. She gave John and Stephenie every option in the store, and she was not afraid to show them her most expensive products. If you start at the bottom like Bill did, you have already lost. Brenda up sold and made sure her client accomplished their goal of updating their house and turning it into their dream home. Imagine how happy Stephenie is with her home after getting all those compliments from her friends. Imagine how happy Brenda is when Stephenie's friends start walking in the door asking for her. Did you catch that? Poor Bill, the rookie, now has to watch Brenda have even more success. Why? Because Brenda knows that **referrals equal success** and she does whatever she can to make sure she receives them.

A friend of mine has owned a bicycle shop for twenty-plus years. When he first started out, times were tough. As well as bicycles, he had to sell picture frames, skis, and anything else he could to pay the bills and to keep the doors open. Today he owns a thriving, successful business. He told me a story that had taken place many years earlier when he had first opened his store. A man walked in his shop on a cold December day, when the bicycle business is typically slow. He had with him two used bikes he had purchased at a second hand store for his two young sons. He had planned on giving his sons the bikes for Christmas since he could not afford to buy new ones. Ryan had to make money when he could, and the repair business was essential to his bottom line, so he gave the man an estimate of what the necessary parts and labor were going to cost. The guy was broke, and didn't have the money to pay for the parts to fix the bikes properly. He asked if Ryan could fix them without the new parts, and if he could just somehow get the bikes in working order. Ryan realized the man just did not have the money to spend on the repairs, and since it was a week before Christmas; he wanted to help him out.

Ryan spent about three hours repairing the bikes without using any new parts. It was a challenge, but he was able to get them into working order. Ryan only charged the man $15 for the repairs. Had he not been in the Christmas spirit, it would have been more like $60. The man paid him and told him when he could afford it, he would be back to purchase his boys each a new bike. Ryan never thought another thing about it, and was happy to have helped a person out who seemed to really need it.

Two years later, a man and woman walked in with two boys looking to purchase a couple of bikes. Once the boys decided what they wanted, without trying to get a better price, the woman wrote out a check. Ryan did not realize this man was the same person he had helped two years before, until he was helping load the bikes into his truck. Two years had passed, and Ryan had forgotten all about that cold December day when he had helped him out. If he had been a jerk, and told him there was nothing he could do, he would not have just sold those two bikes. Right then he realized how important it was for him to be nice to his customers, regardless of the purchase amount. **Being nice pays nice dividends**. He had planned on being in business for many years to come, and being nice to people is one of the reasons he continues to be successful to this day.

Most salespeople sell something their customers can take home and sit on, drive, play, or do something with. They might be buying a new piece of furniture, a new car, or a new video game. My point here is that a consumer, no matter what they purchase, can usually make their purchase and take it home with them. Imagine a sales person who sells something a consumer cannot do any of these things with. Something that they can't see, touch, or do anything with. This invisible item is, you guessed it, *insurance*. A product that none of us seem to be able to live without. Kelly has only been selling insurance for four years, but in that time she has learned the importance of a referral. When she first started in the business, she had to start from ground zero. Her company trained her on their products and services, but she had to provide the customers.

She started out with a list of friends and family that consisted of about 100 names. One at a time, she started filtering through her list by making an appointment with each person, and showing them life insurance and retirement options. When showing them how she could help plan their financial future, her main goal was not just to sell them something. She knew whether they bought anything or not, she needed to get a couple of names on referral. Sure, she was happy if they bought life insurance and opened a retirement account, but without a referral, she would not consider her sale a complete success.

After all, once she filtered through her original list of 100 names, she would not have anyone left to talk to. If every time she did a presentation she received two or three additional referrals, Kelly would never run out of names of people to talk to. She knew going into the insurance business was a numbers game, and the more people she talked to, the more business she would develop. Although not every referral works out, her list of names after four years in the business is consistently over 150. As long as she keeps getting referrals, she will always have people to contact. Even though she does not sell everyone, she succeeds because she receives a referral after every presentation.

When you take the time to get to know your customers, up sell them into better products, and go the extra mile for them, you will get referrals. Even if you do not ask for them, when your client is satisfied with your services, they will tell their friends. Make sure you have a good attitude, tell the truth, read body language, and fix problems when they occur, and you will have many satisfied customers. You will receive referrals as long as you make every effort to make sure your customers are always treated like you would treat your own Grandmother.

*If your Grandmother made a purchase from you, would she be pleased enough to give you a referral?* If you sell good products to your Grandmother, she will give you referral business. Up selling your customers to better products will keep them happier and happy customers will give you referrals without even asking for them. You do not have to sell a consumer a big-ticket item to get a referral. As long as you treat them fair, and sell them a good product, they will be back. Maybe today your customer is only buying a 19" television. Down the road when they are in the market to buy a 50" Plasma, chances are they will be back to buy from you again, as long as you treated them right the first time. You never know when a small purchase will lead to a large one. Treat every customer the same, regardless of the ticket price, and they will undoubtedly send you referral business. Your Grandmother is no different than any other consumer, treat her fair, and you will be rewarded with referrals.

# Part III.

## Selling to Your Grandmother

## Grandma Always Knows Best

Salespeople should always be looking for new ideas and methods to help improve their selling skills. The most common way to acquire this knowledge is through reading books or attending various seminars. With each book you read or each seminar you attend, as long as you learn one new technique that helps improve your sales, it was worth your time.

When a medical student graduates and becomes a doctor, it does not mean that he or she is done being a student. The field of medicine is constantly evolving and changing, and techniques that are used today were not even thought possible 20 years ago. This is why doctors are always attending classes and seminars to learn new skills and new techniques. Whether you are a lawyer studying the changes in the new tax laws, or a sales person training with a new product, people are always learning. As new products are introduced into the marketplace, salespeople must understand how they work in order to properly sell them. To be a successful salesperson, you need to become a student of your business, and it all starts with yourself.

The first time I heard an explanation of Alvin Hansen's *TANSTAAFL theory* was in an economics course in college. The *TANSTAAFL theory* is an acronym for: ***There Ain't No Such Thing As A Free Lunch.*** The theory states that everything has a cost, even if it is supposedly *free*. When people first hear this phrase, they do not want to believe that they cannot get something for free, because everyone hopes to get something for free in his or her lifetime. It might be winning the lottery, or something as small as winning a contest on the radio. Either way, it is something for free. Or is it? To win the lottery, you need to buy the tickets, and to win a radio contest; you have to take the time to call into the radio station. You just cannot get something for nothing; no matter how hard you try. If you were to win a free dinner, you still have to drive to the restaurant, order your meal, and eat it. Sure, it didn't cost you any money, but it did take effort, which means it was not free. I have never forgotten the *TANSTAAFL theory*, and I have always applied it to my life.

My 94 year-old Grandfather once gave me some great words of advice. He told me that in life, you have to go out and make your own success story, and do not expect someone else to make it for you. Just like in the sales profession, you cannot expect to be successful without some effort from yourself. Your sales manager or your fellow salespeople are not going to make you successful; you have to make your own success. Success comes with hard work and dedication, not a *free lunch*.

You always have room for improvement, even if you are the top salesperson at your company. Are you successful? Compared to whom? Just because you are the top salesperson does not mean you cannot increase your sales. If you think you have reached your full potential, ask yourself whom you are comparing yourself to? If you are the most successful person you know compared to your friends and family, than you need to broaden your horizons. Compare yourself to someone like Bill Gates, the founder of Microsoft, or the CEO of Berkshire Hathaway, Warren Buffett. These two men are the wealthiest men in America. Now how successful are you? Toby Keith, country music star, said it best by saying, **"The higher you fly, the bigger targets you make."** You need to reach down inside of yourself and find your untapped potential. Once you do, the sky is the limit.

Tom Brady, quarterback for the New England Patriots, was asked a question following his second Super Bowl victory and his second MVP trophy. A reporter asked him which ring was his favorite? After a short pause, he answered the question by saying his favorite Super Bowl ring was his next one. The next question was how would he be able to start the next season over again with the same intensity as this one? His answer was that he loves training camp and looks forward to improving his skills as an NFL quarterback. This is the same way a salesperson should look at his or her career. Your favorite sale should be your next one and you shouldn't admire your accomplishments for very long. If you do not keep your eyes on the road, you are liable to get into an accident. It is not what you sold yesterday, but what you are going to sell today. As far as training camp, a salesperson should always look forward to bettering and improving themselves, regardless of their previous or current successes.

*Selling to Your Grandmother* teaches you the *Grandmother Philosophy on Sales,* and shows you why you should treat every customer like you would treat your own Grandmother. Now that you have read some things you might be able to do differently in your sales job, what are you going to do? Are you going to put this book back on the shelf and not change anything? How successful are you? How successful do you want to be? Can you improve on your current sales numbers? Like most of us, if you have some areas you need to improve on, now is the time. Try some of the techniques and ideas in *Selling to Your*

*Grandmother* and see if they can make a difference. There is only one way to find out, so go out and try them. **The definition of *insanity* is doing the same thing over and over and expecting a different result.** If you are having trouble during the introduction phase of the sale, you need to try something new. Do not keep doing the same thing you have always been doing if it is not working. The same is true if you are having trouble up selling, or closing the sale. If you get heartburn every time you eat pizza, you can either; get heartburn, stop eating pizza, or take an antacid and eat more pizza. Just like in sales, if you are struggling, you can either; struggle, quit your sales job, or try something new in your selling. The *Grandmother Philosophy* just might be the medicine you have been looking for. The choice is yours.

Tiger Woods is the best golfer in the world; in fact, he is probably the greatest golfer to ever play the game. If you were playing on the PGA tour and wanted to play golf just as good as Tiger, what could you do to improve your game? I suppose the first thing you could do is buy a pair of Nike golf shoes, a Nike hat, and a red Nike shirt. What's next? I almost forgot. You also need to buy a brand new set of golf clubs, exactly the same as Tiger Woods carries in his bag. Now you can go out on the golf course and play just like Tiger. You should be able to hit a perfect 325-yard drive off the tee, straight down the middle of the fairway. You can stick a 150-yard wedge shot within a few feet of the flag, and make birdie or par on every hole. You can wake up now! This all sounds great in theory, but just by having all the same equipment as Tiger will not make you play like Tiger. You would still need to practice. The same is true for a salesperson. Just because something works for someone else, does not mean it will work for you. You have to find out what works for you and what doesn't. To be successful, you have to be constantly looking for and working on new techniques to improve your selling.

While you are looking at ways of improving your career, beware of thinking *the grass is greener on the other side of the fence*. More times than not, jumping the fence is not as simple as it may sound.

The grass *isn't* always greener on the other side of the fence. It sounds like a cliché, but it is true. Sure it might look nicer than your lawn, but is it really? When you are standing in your yard and looking at your grass, it never looks as good as it actually is. Your neighbor's yard on the other side of the fence always seems to look greener, but things are not always as they appear. Sometimes this illusion is because the grass you are looking at is artificial. That's right. Fake grass just like the kind they play football and baseball on in a stadium. Be careful of when someone from another company tries to convince you to work for them. They might try and paint a perfect picture of their company to convince you to jump the fence, but once you make the leap, you realize you were better off before you jumped.

If you have not jumped a fence to realize that your grass was already greener, then ask someone who has. Most will say the grass was greener before they jumped, but by then it was too late to go back. A person jumps a fence by quitting their current job or profession and takes a new job with a different company. Too often they find out they had a better deal before they jumped. If they are not having the success they desire, they think working at a new company will change their success. Although this might occasionally be true, your place of business is not usually the problem. If you are having trouble getting to know your customers, or closing a sale, changing where you work is not going to solve your problems. Before jumping a fence, you should first try applying some of the techniques in *Selling to Your Grandmother* to your selling. Basically, you should water your lawn.

Your yard will look just as good or better than your neighbor's if you nurture it. Feed your mind with books, tapes, and sales seminars to become a better, more successful salesperson. Don't be afraid to try something new. Water and fertilize your lawn with some of the new sales techniques in *Selling to Your Grandmother.* Start treating your customers like you would treat your own Grandmother and watch your grass and your sales grow. Before you know it, you will have the nicest yard in the neighborhood, and you will be on your way to becoming the number one salesperson in your company.

*What If Your Grandmother ...*

*A quick review of the entire book.*

## *If your Grandmother walked into your store, how would you greet her?*

You should never let anything come between you and your customer, especially if that customer is your Grandmother. Don't even for a minute let her walk around your store before greeting her. Get up out of your desk and say hello the moment she walks in the door. If you hesitate, another salesperson might beat you to her. Would you allow another salesperson to sell to your Grandmother? The best time to work with a new customer is when they are in your store; your paperwork and phone calls can wait. Normally you might *FORM* your customer to break the ice, and get them to talk about him or herself. Pay attention to their attire, or what they drove up in, to help guide you with your questions. If you sense some uneasiness with your customer, let them get acclimated to your store before going any further. Do not forget how to handle someone who is "*just looking.*" You might first catch up on recent family events, and then find out what your Granny is looking for. If you imagine your next customer is your Grandmother, you will see how much easier it will be to make a good first impression and connection with them.

*If your Grandmother walked into your store wearing torn up clothes and looking frazzled, would you prejudge her?*

No matter what your Grandmother looks like when she walks into your store, you are still going to treat her like you would treat your own Granny. It doesn't matter whether she looks like she worked all day in her garden, or if she is wearing her best church dress. Even if she drove up in a beat up vehicle, you would still give her the respect she deserves. Just because her hair might look purple, doesn't mean her wallet isn't green. She is there to spend some money no matter what she looks like, and you have no way of knowing how much money she has in her purse, or how much she is willing to spend. Anytime you catch yourself prejudging a consumer, just remember the *Pretty Woman Syndrome*. Successful salespeople do not prejudge their customers. Now think about all the possible situations you can encounter on the sales floor. Now imagine that all those customers' are your Grandmother. How are you going to treat the next consumer who walks into your store? Just like your Grandmother, of course.

## *If your Grandmother walked into your store, would you try to up sell her?*

Your customer is expecting you to be an expert on the products you are selling, and so is your Grandmother. A salesperson needs to be able to give enough information to a consumer for them to be able to make an educated buying decision. If Granny wants to buy the first thing that catches her eye, it doesn't necessarily make it the right product for her. You owe it to your customer to show them the features and benefits of all the products you are selling. Some products are better than others, and it is up to you to make sure they are educated on the differences. Don't forget that the salesperson, the consumer, and the storeowner all benefit from up selling. If you up sell your customers to better products, you will be more likely to do business with them again in the future, and have a customer for life. Satisfied customers equal more referrals. More referrals equal more sales, and more sales equal higher commissions. So the next time you are up selling a customer, treat him or her like you would treat your own Grandmother and try to sell them the best product you can.

*Would you sell your Grandmother a product that you were not proud of or one that you would not buy for yourself?*

You better not. Imagine how upset Granny would be if she found out you sold her something just to make a buck. She might not buy anything from you ever again and she would probably tell all of her friends. The same would be true if one of your clients found out you deceived them. Your Grandmother will trust you more if she knows you own what you are trying to sell her. You must believe you are selling the best product or service in your field, because there is a direct correlation between your belief in your product and your success. You need to own what you sell, and if you wouldn't own it, don't sell it. The only way to be proud of your products is to believe in them and own them. If you believe, you will succeed. Ask a group of salespeople to raise their hands if they own the products they sell. The salespeople with their hands up will be the most successful in the group. If it is not good enough for you, it sure isn't good enough for your Grandmother.

## *How would you go the extra mile for your Grandmother?*

It is the little things that will separate you from your competition and make you successful. If it looks like your Grandmother is worn out from shopping all day, you might offer her a chair and a cold drink. If she called to tell you she put a stain on her new sofa, why not go to your Grandmother's house and remove the stain for her? After all, you would not want your Granny to strain herself. It wouldn't cost you any money to go the extra mile for her, just a little effort. A little effort will go a long way towards your success, so always try to come up with something that will separate you from your competition. Whether you take your clients golfing or fishing, or send them Birthday or Anniversary cards does not matter. It doesn't even matter if you spend any money on your clients, because the intangibles, like staying late with a client after closing, is also going the extra mile. Because there isn't enough time in the day to do all of these things, just pick something to go the extra mile for your clients. No matter what you do, chances are it will pay for itself with the referral business alone. The next time you have a chance to do something extra for a client, imagine that he or she is your Grandmother, and go the extra mile.

## *If you were selling to your Grandmother, how would you close the sale?*

Closing your Grandmother's sale should be an easy task. Don't make it difficult. First off, make sure you ask for the order. Do not let the fear of rejection stop you from making a sale. Your Grandmother, as well as any consumer, is expecting you to ask for the order, so ask. It might surprise you to find out how much business you would close if you would just ask for the order. Also, by assuming your Grandma is only going to buy something from you should make it easier for you to ask. *Keep it simple.* She doesn't expect something for free and she definitely wants you to make a living, so give her your best price and she won't question it. As long as you are giving her a fair deal, you should not have any trouble closing the sale. The next time you are about to ask for an order, ask yourself if you would feel comfortable asking your Grandmother for the same order? If it is good enough for your Granny, it is good enough for your customer.

### *Would you show your Grandmother all of your products even if you could not afford to buy them for yourself?*

Don't limit your sales by only selling the items you can afford. Your Grandmother could have more money than you, so make sure to show her everything you have for sale. Just because you can't afford something, doesn't mean she can't. Consumers have their own wallets, and they might be thicker than yours. If you want to earn larger commission checks, don't limit your sales based on your own income. Make sure you show all of your products to every consumer, regardless of the price tag, because only your consumer knows what they can afford or what they are willing to spend. Remember, if you do not show your Grandmother the products that are out of your own personal price range, someone else will. Another salesperson might get your Grandma's sale, and the commission, because they did not limit their sales based on their own income.

### *Would you keep it simple if your Grandmother walked into your store?*

Now let's suppose that your Grandmother is asking questions about the computers you are selling. How are you going to treat her? If she asks you which kind of computer she needs to buy to be able to send e-mail, what are you going to tell her? I'm sure you are not going to bore her with all the details of the different kinds of computers she could buy. You won't tell her about the size of the hard drive or the speed of the processor. You are going to show her a computer system that will allow her to send e-mail and print pictures of her grand kids. You are going to *keep it simple*. Sure, you could go through all the computer information you know, but it won't impress your Grandmother. The only person who will be impressed with your level of product knowledge is probably yourself. It will only confuse her and make things worse. If your Grandmother happens to be a little more computer savvy than most other Granny's out there, and wants to know about picture editing software, than show her. Just remember to only fire as many bullets as it takes to answer her questions. Imagine your next customer is your Grandmother. How will you keep it simple?

## *If your Grandmother walked into your store, would you have a good attitude?*

If you didn't already have a smile on your face, you should have one now. You do not want your Grandmother to know that you are having a bad day. Even though you may want to tell her you got a flat tire on the way to work, you won't. You want her to be in the best possible mood while shopping in your store. For Grandma to open her checkbook and give you money, she needs to be happy. If she is depressed because you just told her your dog died, you will probably lose the sale. Don't do or say anything to put a damper on your customers' spirits. Unhappy people generally don't spend money. They came into your store to buy something, so keep them in the buying mood with a good attitude. Besides, why would anyone want to put his or her Grandmother in a bad mood?

## *If your Grandmother walked into your store, would you tell her the truth?*

When you were a kid, do you think your Grandmother knew when you were telling her a story? She probably not only knew when you were lying, but she knew it before you even opened your mouth. If you imagine that your customer is your Grandmother, you would probably tell the truth, the whole truth, and nothing but the truth. You wouldn't even chance it. Do you know anyone who could pull one over on his or her Grandmother? I can't stand finding out I was lied to, and neither can your consumers. The point here is simple, just tell the truth and you will stay out of trouble. Don't make up a crazy story to sound good in front of your customer. Make sure your story is the truth, and don't be afraid to tell it. The moment of truth is a good thing for an honest salesperson. As long as you have your consumer's best interest at heart, don't worry. Like Grandmothers, most consumers are able to separate fact from fiction. If you lie to your customers, the only truth will be that your competition will win over your customer and their business.

***If your Grandmother walked into your store, how
would you read her body language?***

It is important to watch for the different expressions
on your Grandmother's face while she is shopping in your
store.  If you are explaining the features and benefits of a
product, her face is a good indicator to see if she understands
what you are saying.  If her eyes are glazing over, you may
have confused her.  If you don't go back and find where you
lost her, Granny will probably get irritated, and chances are
she won't buy what you are trying to sell her.  Facial
expressions, posture, and the tone of a persons' voice are all
types of body language that a salesperson needs to pay
attention to.  You should always be watching for these silent
signals to know if your customer is with you or not.  Picture
your Grandmother's face when she caught you sneaking a
cookie from her cookie jar.  Now think of that face as a
reminder to never forget to pay attention to your customer's
body language.

## *If your Grandmother walked into your store with a problem, how would you fix it?*

You should try to keep your Grandmother as happy as possible if she encounters a problem. They are never any fun, but problems do give you an opportunity to excel and to show your customer just how good you really are at your job. If your Grandmother has a problem, take care of it quickly and painlessly. If she is having engine trouble with the new car she just purchased from you, make sure she gets your best loaner car until hers is fixed. If your customer were your Grandmother, how would you accommodate her? When you have a problem, try to find a way to make it a positive for both you and your customer. When you fix a problem, and make your customer happy, they will probably remember you more than if they didn't have a problem in the first place. Because problems are going to happen, you might as well embrace them, and fix them as if your customer were your own Grandmother.

## *If your Grandmother walked into your store, would she buy from you?*

You would not show up at your Grandmother's house looking like you had been out all night and didn't have time for a shower. You also wouldn't have food in your teeth or coffee breath. Not a chance. You would make sure your hair was nice, your clothes were clean, and your teeth were brushed. The next time you are going to work, look in the mirror. Ask yourself if you saw your Grandmother today, would she be proud of her Grandson or Granddaughter? If the answer is yes, than get on the sales floor and set a new sales record. If the answer is no, get your act together. If you look successful, you will feel successful, and if you feel successful, you will be successful. Make sure to keep your act clean, so you can clean up on your competition. Just like when you were a kid, you should always try to make your Grandmother proud.

*If your Grandmother made a purchase from you, would she be pleased enough to give you a referral?*

If you sell good products to your Grandmother, she will give you referral business. Up selling your customers to better products will keep them happier and happy customers will give you referrals without even asking for them. You don't have to sell a consumer a big-ticket item to get a referral. As long as you treat them fair, and sell them a good product, they will be back. Maybe today your customer is only buying a 19" television. Down the road when they are in the market to buy a 50" Plasma, chances are they will be back to buy from you again, as long as you treated them right the first time. You never know when a small purchase will lead to a large one. Treat every consumer the same, regardless of the ticket price, and they will undoubtedly send you referral business. Your Grandmother is no different than any other consumer, treat her fair, and you will be rewarded with referrals.

*Remember, Grandma always knows best ...*

*... when it comes to*

## *" SELLING TO YOUR GRANDMOTHER"*

For more information, please visit
www.sellingtoyourgrandmother.com

## About the Author and Illustrator

Chris has worked in the sales industry for over 13 years, in both wholesale and retail, where he has held various management positions and attained numerous sales awards. He has worked as a corporate sales trainer and as a sales and marketing consultant to various retail businesses, as well as manufacturers. Chris attended the University of Montana with an emphasis on Business and Marketing. He is married with two children, and takes an active role in his community, as well as volunteering his time to local charities.

Joel is a long time freelance illustrator and a graduate of the Chouinard Art Institute. He belongs to the Society of Illustrators and the Art Directors Club in Los Angeles, as well as the Technical Illustrators Management, Editorial Art, and the Magazine Editors Associations. Today, he spends most of his time between his studio and his fishing boat. If you don't find him with a pencil in his hand, he is probably holding a fishing pole somewhere out in the Pacific Ocean. Stop by and visit him at www.joelbarbee.com

# ABOUT THE AUTHOR

 David Borenstein, M.D., is clinical professor of medicine and former medical director of the Spine Center and the George Washington University Medical Center. Dr. Borenstein is a board-certified internist and rheumatologist who is internationally recognized for his expertise in the care of patients with back pain and spinal disorders.

Dr. Borenstein received his undergraduate degree from Columbia University in 1969. His medical school, internal medicine residency, and rheumatology fellowship training were completed at the Johns Hopkins University Medical School and Hospital from 1969 to 1978. he became an assistant professor of medicine at the George Washington University Medical Center in 1978. He was promoted to professor of medicine in 1989. He became a clinical professor of medicine on the voluntary faculty in 1997.

Dr. Borenstein is an author of a number of medical articles and books, including *Low Back Pain: Medical Diagnosis and Comprehensive Management (2nd ed.)*. This book has been recognized by the Medical Library Association Brandon/Hill list as one of the 200 essential books for a medical library. He is also author of *Neck Pain: Medical Diagnosis and Management*. He has lectured to the general public on behalf of the Arthritis Foundation on a wide variety of medical topics. He has chaired low back pain symposia for a number of physician groups, including the American College of Rheumatology. He has also moderated national telesymposia sponsored by pharmaceutical companies for physicians. He has also served as a medical guest expert for CNN and local news programs.

Dr. Borenstein is a fellow of the American College of Physicians and American College of Rheumatology. He is a member of the International Society for the Study of the Lumbar Spine and is listed in The Best Doctors in America, Year 200 Edition. He is included in *Who's Who in Medicine and Healthcare, 2nd edition* and *Who's Who in America, 54th edition*. He is in active clinical practice in Washington, D.C.